125 YEARS

EX SOLO AD SOLEM

A HISTORY OF
THE BRYN MAWR SCHOOL

by Elizabeth Nye Di Cataldo

Title page: Junior class showers
seniors with daisies, 2007

Published by The Bryn Mawr School
109 West Melrose Avenue
Baltimore, Maryland 21210

Design: Karen Wright

Printing: Schmitz Press

ISBN 978-0-615-46965-2

The Bryn Mawr School is an independent, nonsectarian, college-preparatory school for girls from preschool through grade twelve. Within a nurturing environment, Bryn Mawr's rigorous academic curriculum inspires a passion for intellectual curiosity and emphasizes the delights and demands of learning. In the classical humanistic tradition, Bryn Mawr promotes the full development of mind, body, and spirit. The school cultivates respect for diversity and engenders habits of moral and ethical leadership and a sense of responsibility to the broader community.

A Bryn Mawr education is grounded in the expectation that young women will be resilient in the face of complexity, ambiguity, and change; will become responsible and confident participants in the world; and will lead considered and consequential lives.

Mission Statement of The Bryn Mawr School in 2011

Contents

Foreword

Throughout our celebrations of The Bryn Mawr School's 125th anniversary, we have been reminded of the foresight and determination of our five founding women, as well as the women who have led the school through the years since. Bryn Mawr began with an auspicious purpose, dedicated to providing young girls and women with opportunities never before available to them. The school's original mission of challenging students to question, to achieve, and to become passionate about lifelong learning has never wavered over our long history, and our purpose has remained unchanged for the generations of young women who have passed through our doors. Through our history, Bryn Mawr has asked girls to "take the test" by raising their own expectations of their capabilities, whether it is in the classroom, on the stage, in the studio, or on a playing field. Hundreds of talented and devoted teachers and coaches have led thousands of spirited girls through Bryn Mawr's academic and extracurricular programs over the years. But it is the quieter message they convey, the moment when a student becomes aware of her own capacity, often through hard work and perseverance, to solve a dilemma, master a theory, or perfect a shot, that has always been the essence of Bryn Mawr.

We are Edith Hamilton's school. Her vision for the intellectual life as the center of the academic program at Bryn Mawr continues. While contemporary Bryn Mawr girls do not resemble those Victorian-clad young ladies of so long ago, their love of the demands and delights of learning, of challenge, and of spirit, are truly the same. I believe that Miss Hamilton would walk the halls of any building on our campus and be delighted at the frank and often excited conversations within, where faculty and students work their way through a problem and arrive at a solution that they may never have anticipated. Creativity flows from art studio to computer lab, and physical expression happens in the gymnasiums, the dance studio, and on the playgrounds. I think she would be proud of us all.

The Bryn Mawr School continues to celebrate the life of the mind, the creative spirit, the compelling sense of service to the community and the world, and the commitment to developing young woman who are resilient, confident, and engaged in a considered and consequential life. We salute our important role Bryn Mawr School has played in the history of women's education, and we look forward to our future with confidence and much pride.

Maureen E. Walsh
Headmistress

Preface

As I began my research for Ex *Solo Ad Solem*, I discovered a wealth of material about the history of the school. Newspaper and journal articles, books and diaries, oral histories, and hand-written memories have been recently digitized and made easily accessible. With such a substantial collection of information, I chose to write Bryn Mawr's history as a documented account, describing the school's development within the context of its mission and the events which shaped it over the years. There are many wonderful stories yet to be told about Bryn Mawr. My hope is that this book can provide the background and framework for those stories.

I was greatly assisted in my research by archivists and special collections librarians, including Barbara Grubb, Marianne Hansen, and Lorette Treese at Bryn Mawr College; Jim Stimpert at Johns Hopkins University; Gwen Erickson at Guilford College; Anne Thomson at Newnham College, Cambridge University; the librarians at Goucher and Vassar Colleges; archivists Nancy Gilpin at Gilman, Dante Beretta at Garrison Forest, and Michelle Feller-Koffman at Park; and numerous dedicated librarians at the Maryland Historical Society and the Maryland Room at the Enoch Pratt Free Library. Kathy Waters Sander, biographer of Mary Elizabeth Garrett, has been both generous and supportive. Of course, all errors and omissions in this work are purely my own.

My most sincere thanks go to Headmistress Maureen Walsh for entrusting me with this wonderful opportunity to explore and share Bryn Mawr's fascinating history. I am also thankful to Associate Headmistress Peggy Bessent for bringing me into Bryn Mawr's archives and this community of people passionate about scholarship and the ideals of lifelong learning and leadership for women. I am most grateful for conversations with many alumnae, but most particularly for the insights and support of Nancy Ratcliffe Ferrell '75, Jennie Lee Williams Fowlkes '65, and Betsy Strobel Wilgis '58, as well as those of former headmistresses Blair Stambaugh and Barbara Landis Chase, all remarkable women who have been fundamental to Bryn Mawr's success for the last several decades. Nancy Sherman, a superb editor, and designer Karen Wright patiently and carefully brought the book together. My attentive readers, particularly Diane Levine, Arna Margolis, Julie Smith Marshall '89, Suzy Feldman Rosenthal '72, Kris Schaffner '93, Mary Armstrong Shoemaker '69, and Susan Solberg, were masters with both a red pen and encouragement. I would also like to thank my mother, Nan Nye, as well as my own Bryn Mawr girls, Sandra and Juliana, Classes of 2012 and 2016, for their patience and understanding during the many long months of research and writing.

Elizabeth Nye Di Cataldo

hat your last le...

...ve me. In estab...

...is new school y...

...oing something...

...as never yet be...

...one in Boston.

...have no private p...

...tory school for g...

...far as I know.

...irls' Latin School

...ublic and Cha...

...Hall School is f...

...nd girls, while...

...many private schools

...annot and do not do

have

which

impor

n ef-

county

beg

ve

der

hin

my satisfaction in your

announcement concern...

...the salaries and

Chapter One

ON THE SAME TERMS AS MEN 1885–1896

·THE· BRYN· MAWR· SCHOOLHOUSE· BALTIMORE· MD·
·HENRY· RUTGERS· MARSHALL· ARCH'T·

*T*he Bryn Mawr School was founded in 1885 by five young Baltimore women determined to provide girls with an education equal to the best available to boys at the time. M. Carey Thomas, Mary Elizabeth Garrett, Mamie Gwinn, Bessie King, and Julia Rogers resolved not only to provide the education they themselves had desired, but also to raise the standards of girls' education to meet the rigorous expectations of admission to Bryn Mawr College. Their intelligence, determination, social standing, and influence made them uniquely prepared for their mission.

During their childhood in Baltimore at the close of the Civil War, boys of families of means could attend local private schools in preparation for boarding schools and such colleges as Harvard, Princeton, and Yale. There were few opportunities for girls to go to college, and little desire of these same families to prepare their daughters for academic rigor beyond the finishing school curriculum of languages, poetry, literature, and the arts. Girls were often tutored at home and then sent to local schools run by Civil War widows or other women who had received little more than a finishing school education themselves. Girls were expected to prepare for marriage, to support and assist their husbands in their business affairs, to manage households and raise the children, and perhaps to contribute their services and skills to charitable work in their communities. For a girl who desired a more intellectual life, these limited expectations would prove quite frustrating. Fortunately, for girls in Baltimore and nationwide, these five strong women chose to challenge convention and had the means to do so.

M. Carey Thomas, daughter of influential Orthodox Quaker leaders Dr. James Carey Thomas and Mary Whitall Thomas, was the first woman to graduate Phi Beta Kappa from Cornell University in 1877, after only two years of study. She was permitted to study the classics with Dr. Basil Gildersleeve at The Johns Hopkins University, but was restricted from attending lectures and seminars with the male students. The university would not guarantee that she

> "I got perfectly enraged: how unjust–how narrow-minded, how utterly incomprehensible to deny that women ought to be educated and worse than all to deny that they have equal powers of mind. If I ever live and grow up, my one aim and concentrated purpose shall be and is to show that a woman can learn, can reason, can compete with men in the grand fields of literature and science and conjecture that opens before the nineteenth century."
>
> *M. Carey Thomas, writing in her journal at age 14*

M. Carey Thomas

could receive a graduate degree, and she withdrew the next year in frustration. M. Carey Thomas then convinced her father to allow her to travel to Germany to continue her studies. In 1883, following attempts at two previous European universities, she was the first American woman to receive a doctorate from the University of Zurich, and was the first woman ever to be awarded a doctorate summa cum laude from the university. With assistance from family members who served as trustees at the newly forming Bryn Mawr College, Thomas was named dean of faculty and professor of English in 1884, but not given the presidency that she desired. In her indomitable way, she convinced the board to raise educational standards for women to a level of excellence never before established, and personally oversaw the development of a curriculum that closely resembled the rigorous research-based methods of the great European universities. As her father, her cousin Francis T. King, and their friend John W. Garrett had done as founding board members of The Johns Hopkins University in Baltimore, she strove to raise American standards of both undergraduate and graduate education, but she did so for women. Her unprecedented credentials provided her with insight into the best of the educational world and the ability to speak with an authority that other women lacked. While she was not experienced either in teaching or in school administration, she quickly acquired the necessary skills to put her theories into practice.

Mary Elizabeth Garrett

Mary Elizabeth Garrett had become one of the wealthiest unmarried women in the country in 1884, when her father, John Work Garrett, president of the Baltimore and Ohio Railroad, left to her a share of his estate equal to that of her two older brothers, contrary to customs of the day. She had attended the fashionable Baltimore girls' finishing school run by Miss Sarah Agnes Kummer near her home on Mount Vernon Place, but noted in her journal her disappointment to find it based upon "cultivation, not college." After she left the school at the age of seventeen, she studied privately as did many young women at the time. She attempted but did not pass the Harvard Examinations for Women in 1879 and did not pursue any further formal education. She continued to hire tutors, attended many lectures and seminars, and traveled frequently with her family throughout Europe, where she studied art and culture. She became "Papa's secretary" as she assisted her father for years, and was often by his side at business meetings with some of the great industrialists of the time as they planned and negotiated. She acquired a keen business acumen that, through guarded philanthropy, would enable her to affect change for both women and education on a national level.

Mary MacKall Gwinn

Elizabeth Tabor King

Mamie Gwinn, the daughter of the attorney general of the state of Maryland and the niece of influential United States senator Reverdy Johnson, traveled with M. Carey Thomas to study in Europe. She eventually withdrew from the male-dominated University of Leipzig and continued to study privately for eight to ten hours a day for several years. She assisted Thomas in her writing and in crafting the original curriculum for Bryn Mawr College. She was the first doctoral student of the college and served as professor of English there for several years.

Neither Bessie King nor Julia Rogers obtained college degrees. Bessie King was often ill and probably suffered from tuberculosis. Her father, Francis T. King, dedicated much of his life to the improvement of education and sat on the boards of many institutions, including those of The Johns Hopkins University and Hospital, Haverford and Bryn Mawr Colleges, and Baltimore's Manual Labor School. After several years at Miss Kummer's school, in 1872 he sent Bessie to the Howland Institute, a Quaker boarding school for girls in Union Springs, New York, with her cousin M. Carey Thomas. When Bessie returned to Baltimore she studied privately, hoping to enter the new Johns Hopkins University as an undergraduate, but was disappointed to find that women would not be admitted.

Julia Rebecca Rogers

Julia Rogers also studied privately after leaving Miss Kummer's school, and in June of 1879 was one of only eight women nationwide to pass the Harvard Exam and receive a certificate of her success.[1] In 1881, she read Greek and Latin at Newnham College in Cambridge, England, but did not return to continue her studies. As both her parents had died, she lived with her mother's elder Baltimore relatives, and was the only founder of The Bryn Mawr School whose father did not serve as a trustee at either the college or at Johns Hopkins. There is some indication that she may have been a ward of John W. Garrett in her youth. She often traveled abroad with Mary Elizabeth Garrett and her family.[2]

These five young friends began to meet twice a month in the late 1870s, calling themselves "the Friday Night."[3] They discussed literature, philosophy, art, and theater, and they attempted to write their own novel as a group. The book was soon abandoned, however, as they turned their attention instead to finding practical solutions for the educational and societal problems of girls and young women of the day.

As she considered the future consequences for women's education while drafting policy for Bryn Mawr College, M. Carey Thomas realized that the college should not include a preparatory division, as Vassar and The Women's College of Baltimore (later Goucher College) had done. Bryn Mawr College was to be an institution dedicated to higher learning, with a graduate program and fellowships to inspire younger women to continue on to advanced work. Thomas deliberately crafted the undergraduate entrance examinations to the college to be as difficult as the exams for the best men's colleges, even though she was aware that few girls would be prepared to pass them, much less thrive under the rigor of the curriculum once they did. Most young girls either studied with tutors or attended schools more interested in finishing them for society and marriage than for intellectual endeavors. In her 1883 letter to Dr. James Rhoads, who was responsible for the formation of the Quaker college, Thomas had written that "since the absence of the regularly organized preparatory schools that exist for boys greatly embarrasses a girl who means to enter college, I consider it very important that a year, or if possible two years before the opening of Bryn Mawr, there should be sent to all the Friends' schools, and published in the Nation and in all the leading journals, a full list, made out by the president and such professors as shall be already appointed, of the entrance requirements."[4] This would provide girls and their teachers with a set of established standards for their studies, as the Harvard Examinations For Women had done, but with the goal of entering a college specifically created for intelligent women.

In the spring of 1885, the board of Bryn Mawr College agreed to allow M. Carey Thomas and her friends to use the college's name to establish a girls' preparatory school in Baltimore.[5] Just as they had watched the formation of the college with keen interest, male and female academics across the country quickly began to write their encouragement and to suggest their own graduates and young teachers as faculty for the new school. Letters of recommendation and requests from applicants referred to their desire to be part of this new endeavor, which would also further their own studies and careers.[6] Working at The Bryn Mawr School was seen as validation of their work and ability and as a guarantee of their future academic success. The founders, now calling themselves the "Committee," took great care in choosing the faculty for their school and insisted that teachers had degrees "from some college of good standing."[7] Each academic subject would be taught by women who not only had graduated from fine programs, but who had distinguished themselves as both scholars and capable teachers.[8] Many had begun advanced studies in European universities, but few could obtain graduate degrees from them.

After studying both girls' schools and women's colleges throughout the Northeast and the Mid-Atlantic regions, the Committee established several fundamental criteria for the new school. As stated in the first Bryn Mawr School catalog, students would be prepared for "the highest requirements for entrance made by any college" by their study of "Latin, French, mathematics, history and English, and science, throughout the course; and either Greek or German, from the fourth year onward." The older students would have laboratory science, while the younger girls would "receive oral instruction in the elements of botany, zoology and mineralogy" and would draw specimens from the school's collections. Elocution and drawing were obligatory. Beyond passing the requirements of their own teachers, the students were regularly examined by professors from Johns Hopkins, Cornell, and Bryn Mawr College to ensure that they were being properly instructed and prepared for entrance to college. Completion of the program required successfully finishing the coursework as well as passing the Bryn Mawr College entrance exams in the last two years of their studies, whether they intended to go to college or not.[9] Parents who might be concerned about the rigor of the curriculum were assured that any child of "average capacity and average health" could undertake the program. Homework would be "strictly limited," but parents also were informed that because the studies proceeded

The first school building near the corner of Eutaw and Monument Streets, was adjacent to the physics building of Johns Hopkins University, where Hopkins men could observe Bryn Mawr girls at work in their science lab, thus earning the school the name of "Little Miss Hopkins."

at a fixed rate, "any pupil who through absence or lack of diligence had failed to complete her year's work satisfactorily" would not move forward.[10]

The Committee was aware that it was "offering the people of Baltimore what they [did] not want: a first class college preparatory education for girls," as Headmistress Edith Hamilton would write to M. Carey Thomas in 1915.[11] They also were fighting the scientific reasoning of Dr. Edward H. Clarke, a prominent Boston physician against equal education for young girls. In his 1873 book, *Sex in Education*, Clarke declared that it was against the very laws of nature and physiology, "a crime before God and humanity," for women to be educated as men were.[12] He argued that, while women were capable of intellectual study, their education occurred during the same time that their reproductive organs were developing. Since the physical body could not do more than one thing well at a time (he used the example of reading poetry and operating a saw concurrently), the work of the brain that education required would detract from the bodily forces and the flow of blood needed for complete formation of those organs essential to the reproduction and survival of the human race. His book was so popular that it sold out in less than a week and would run through seventeen editions in fifteen years. His theories were eventually dispelled as college-educated women gave birth to healthy, robust babies, but as M. Carey Thomas said thirty-five years later: "We did not know when we began whether women's health could stand the strains of education. We were haunted in those days by the clanging chains of that gloomy little spector, Dr. Edward H. Clarke's *Sex in Education*."[13] The fear that the study of Latin could cause sterility continued among some members of the Baltimore community well past 1885 and the founding of both Bryn Mawr institutions.

On September 21, 1885, two dozen young girls of varying educational backgrounds and seven very highly educated and dedicated female teachers entered the doors of the former Friends' Academy (next to the Quaker meetinghouse at 715 N. Eutaw Street) and began a new era in girls' education.[14] It would take some time

THE BRYN MAWR SCHOOL

to be opened September 21st, 1885.

MISS ALICE GODDARD,   LATIN AND GREEK.
A. B., Cornell University. Studied Zurich and Oxford, 1884–85.

MISS CHARLOTTE SMITH,   MATHEMATICS.
Ph. B., Cornell University. (1885.)

Miss Marcella Oready (*To be appointed later.*)   SCIENCE.

MISS MARY S. LOCKE,   HISTORY AND ENGLISH.
A. B., Smith College.

MISS ELEANOR A. ANDREWS, *Secretary,*   ENGLISH.
In residence at Newnham College, Cambridge, England, 1880 and 1882.

MR. HUGH NEWELL,   DRAWING.
Instructor in Drawing, Johns Hopkins University.

MR. CHARLES L. WOODWORTH, JR.,   ELOCUTION.
Instructor in Elocution, Johns Hopkins University.

Teachers of French and German will be appointed at a later date.

Reading, writing, arithmetic through long division, and elementary geography, are required for admission to the school.

The prescribed course is such as can be taken by any child of average capacity and average health, and the number of daily lessons requiring preparation will be strictly limited.

Drawing and elocution are obligatory.

There will be a laboratory for the use of the older pupils in science; the younger pupils will receive oral instruction in the elements of botany, zoölogy and mineralogy, and will learn to make drawings from specimens furnished them.

A small library of books of reference will be attached to the school.

The course of instruction is the same for all pupils; it proceeds by fixed and gradual stages, and it should be understood that any pupil who through absence or lack of diligence has failed

First school catalog in 1885

Postcard of the school at Cathedral Street, 1909

"... we knew simply and without question that Bryn Mawr was the best. Others could be finishing schools . . . or country style boarding schools . . . ; they could teach manners, art, piano, horsemanship; we were all out for brains. Other schools might believe in being bright, colorful, attractive, warm; Bryn Mawr believed in being Important. Bryn Mawr School girls went to college; or if they didn't, no matter; they were educated as though they were going."

Mary H. (Bebe) Cadwalader, Class of 1934, Baltimore Evening Sun, *December 2, 1972*

for the teachers to test and determine the different levels of academic preparation of the girls, and for several years the students would range between the ages of eight and twenty. It was three years before the first two older girls were recognized as having been fully prepared to go on to college. By 1891, when Leonie Gilmour was awarded the first full scholarship to Bryn Mawr College, only six girls had made it through successfully. In the early years, many girls would leave without completing the curriculum or passing the college's entrance exams, but were proud that they had done as well as they had in a school that "stood for brains."[15]

By 1888, the success of the school seemed assured, and the quickly growing student body would soon need larger quarters with much better facilities. The founders had aspirations for their students that could not be met in the cramped confines of the former Friends' Academy. Mary Elizabeth Garrett hired Henry Rutgers Marshall, the New York architect who had designed the schoolhouse for The Brearley School in Manhattan and the renovations of her own Mount Vernon home, to design the ideal city school building. The triangular lot that she purchased at the corner of Cathedral and Preston Streets was a former coal yard surrounded by lumberyards, sawmills, and a variety of carpenters' shops. It was, however, strategically located between the mansions of Mount Vernon Place and the more recently built townhomes on Eutaw Place and in Bolton Hill. Although Mary Garrett preferred to remain a private person, news of her financing and supervision of the construction of a very unique school building in Baltimore soon made the pages of newspapers throughout the country, with speculation that the cost would be more than $200,000. The actual cost to her would be closer to $400,000 when the building was completed and furnished, about $9.3 million in the currency of 2010.[16]

The building was massive; ninety feet across, seventy feet deep, and eighty feet high from the pavement to the peak of the dark terracotta tiled roof. A high brick wall blocked prying eyes from the cement "garden" behind the building, where Bryn Mawr girls would soon play tennis and basketball on outdoor courts. The lower level of the building was faced with huge slabs of rough-faced dark brown North Carolina sandstone, many pieces weighing several tons. The upper stories were a study in shades of brown Pompeian brick, never before seen in Baltimore, but quickly copied by the local brickmakers.[17] Decorative patterns included a band that ran across the face of the building and a mosaic over the door that read "Bryn Mawr School, 1888–1889" to mark the dates of construction. Below, six wide steps led from the sidewalk to the entranceway, where students passed over another Bryn Mawr mosaic, this one in colored stone.[18] This same mosaic is installed today in front of the Owlgate, between the Garrett and Hamilton buildings, thanks to the efforts of a group of dedicated alumnae.

Inside the school, light from an enormous dormer gleamed on glazed Ingram tiles imported from the famous Wortley Brick Works in Leeds, England. An immense iron double staircase with slate steps and landings and exquisitely crafted iron railings commanded the center of the building. On the lower level was a gymnasium with a running track suspended above the latest equipment ordered by Dr. Kate Hurd, "who ha[d] been especially fitting herself for her work in the school by studying under Dr. Sargent and in the schools of Sweden, Germany, and London."[19] Next to the gymnasium were a locker room, showers (referred to as "needle baths"), dressing rooms, and one of the earliest indoor swimming pools in a school anywhere in the country. Above the gymnasium was a well-stocked library with an iron gallery around the upper walls to add more shelf space, as well as four large classrooms. Over the pool and dressing rooms was "one large room, the use of which is seen in few other schools. It is called a 'silent study-room,' and accommodates 150 pupils, the number for which the school has been built. Every girl will have her own desk in this room, which will be devoted to study alone without the unpleasant interruption occasioned by recitations going on at the same time."

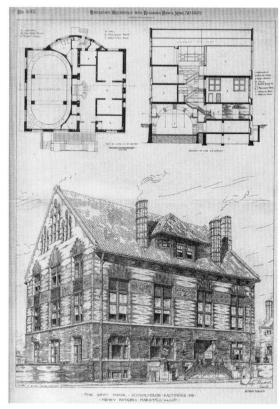

American Architect, *March 30, 1889*

"No child could walk through that heavy, iron-studded front door (which closed with a click-swuush!) without sensing that the building Stood For Something."

Mary H. Cadwalader, Class of 1934

First and second primary classes in the gymnasium

Girls were taught to swim with the assistance of a pulley on the ceiling

Up another flight of the massive stairs was an art room graced with natural light from skylights, and a science laboratory with walls covered in blue and gray glazed tile and an asphalt floor to resist the "fumes of the chemicals."[20] Fire, which had and would continue to devastate Baltimore through the years, would not be a problem in this building, as only the doors, windows, and furnishings were wooden. The entire structure was composed of iron, steel, brick, stone, tile, and cement. When a fire raged directly across the street, destroying a two-story planing mill filled with wood on October 6, 1892, the front wall of the school became so hot that the firemen had to turn their hoses on it. The expensive plate glass windows cracked, but the school sustained no other damage. Neighboring buildings, including the Lyceum Theatre, did not fare as well. The firemen were well taken care of that day, as "[t]he ladies of the school . . . supplied the firemen with hot coffee and sandwiches."[21]

While construction was under way, Mary Garrett was collecting the artwork that she hoped would inspire the students throughout their day at school. The hallways, classrooms, and study hall were filled, in true Victorian fashion, with plaster casts of classical, European, and American statuary and reliefs, including a replica of the Parthenon frieze that encircled the walls of the study hall. The classrooms were adorned with paintings and lithographs related to the subjects taught in them. Hawthorne and Tennyson hung in the English room, Galileo adorned mathematics, and a large variety of bas-relief architectural details covered the walls of the art room for the girls to study and draw.[22]

"It is more than doubtful," wrote journalist Lucy Bull in The Critic, "if any other preparatory school in the country has so generous a collection of Braun autotypes of the most famous paintings, to say nothing of the chromolithographs by the Arundel Society of London."[23]

At the World's Columbian Exposition in Chicago in 1893, the school won a blue ribbon for its large exhibit complete with curriculum displays and a custom-made wooden model of the school building. Karl Baedeker gave the "tasteful" structure a star in the 1899 edition of his guidebook of the United States.[24]

Finally, Bryn Mawr had the quarters it needed to fulfill its bold educational mission for young girls and women and to set an example for other schools to follow. Once the school moved into its new building, Mary Elizabeth Garrett and the other founders could focus on other matters of utmost importance to the women's cause.

The Johns Hopkins University had opened in 1876, and construction had begun on the thirteen buildings of the hospital complex in 1877. Nine years later the hospital still was not finished, and there were no finalized plans for the long-awaited medical school that was to accompany it. Johns Hopkins' bequest was funded directly by

Silent study hall, circa 1900

income generated from stock of the B&O Railroad, now in financial distress without the firm hand of John W. Garrett to preside over it. President Daniel Coit Gilman had severely limited funds to keep the university running at the standards expected of it, to finish the costly hospital construction, and to open a medical school. The only recourse would be to find a wealthy donor to supplement the dwindling medical school funds. Gilman assured the trustees in 1888 that "a man of large means" would certainly step forward to provide the $100,000 needed, for whom they would name the medical school.[25]

When the hospital finally opened on May 7, 1889, with invited guests crowding through the doors at the celebrations while onlookers stood at the gates, the medical school was still floundering.[26] Mary Garrett and her friends saw an opportunity to advance women's medical education, but they would have to move quickly. They knew Gilman needed $100,000 to begin building and was looking for a man to provide it. If they could raise the necessary funds first, they might elicit from him a promise to meet their contingencies, the most essential of which was the admission of women to the medical school. The Bryn Mawr School founders planned a national campaign and quietly gathered committees of influential women including the first lady, Caroline Harrison, who headed the Washington, D.C. committee. They wrote letters, held gatherings, and convinced women and men nationwide to contribute. In October, 1889, they learned that Gilman had told trustees that at least $500,000 would be necessary before they could open the medical school, fully five times the initial goal. Mary Garrett stepped forward with the balance needed to reach the first $100,000, so that they could secure the promise of admission of women that would provide the impetus needed to raise the rest. An earnest national public campaign for the Women's Fund for the Medical School began with a lavish party for fifteen hundred guests at Mary Garrett's Mount Vernon Place mansion, at which the first lady served as hostess.[27]

Julia Rogers was not at this event, and by this time had left the group, resigned from the board of managers of The Bryn Mawr School, and moved on to other interests, notably the suffrage movement. After twenty years of friendship with Mary Garrett, they agreed to purge their former correspondence and are not noted together again at social functions. Conflicts over decisions about the running of the school, as well as friction over relationships among the women, had grown too difficult for them to continue working together. Although the initial public meeting for the medical school fund had been held in Bessie King's parlor on May 2, 1890, she also withdrew from the group at the height of the medical school campaign in 1891. Her father, Francis T. King, had died, and as he had been opposed to coeducation at the medical school of which he was president of the board, she may have felt that she could not continue to campaign for it. Her chronic illnesses were also taking a toll on her, but did not keep her from working for women's political advancement in the future.[28]

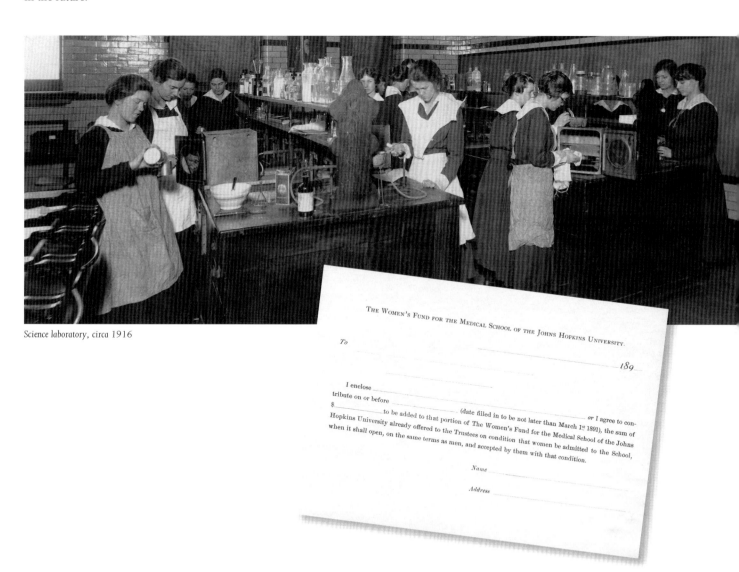

Science laboratory, circa 1916

THE WOMEN'S FUND FOR THE MEDICAL SCHOOL OF THE JOHNS HOPKINS UNIVERSITY.

To

189

I enclose

tribute on or before

$ (date filled in to be not later than March 1st 1891), the sum of to be added to that portion of The Women's Fund for the Medical School of the Johns Hopkins University already offered to the Trustees on condition that women be admitted to the School, when it shall open, on the same terms as men, and accepted by them with that condition.

Name

Address

In frustration, in the spring of 1891 Mary Garrett offered another $100,000 of her own money toward the medical school, if the trustees themselves could raise the balance of $220,000 by February of 1892. She then left the country for a year and a half, and extended the trustees' due date indefinitely. On her return, M. Carey Thomas informed her of a potentially disastrous power struggle between the university and the hospital over the medical school. Mary chose to take drastic and immediate action and offered to pay the entire remaining sum of more than $300,000 herself, but with stringent conditions attached. Not only would the medical school have to admit women "on the same terms as men," but a building was to be named in recognition of the donors, the Women's Fund Memorial Building. The admission of women on the same terms as men was to be printed on every circular or calendar, and an oversight committee of her choice would assist the women of the school. Most important for the future of medical education in America, she stipulated that the medical school would be a four-year graduate institution, similar to European medical schools. Applicants would be required to have a background in French, German, physics, chemistry, and biology in their college education. Thus, she was making a formal stipulation that the preliminary medical course created earlier by the faculty of the university be instated as the minimum requirement to enter the medical school. Few students had successfully completed the courses over the years since 1878.[29] She also insisted that the school be opened by the fall of 1893, giving the board mere months to take action. The board met hurriedly, without Gilman, who was out of town, and accepted her gift and her terms. For the next month they tried to convince her to change the difficult admissions criteria, but she would not budge. In February of 1893 they came to a final agreement to her terms.[30]

Dr. Gilman, in announcing the agreement in February of 1893, indicated how far news had spread: "Indeed, a lady writing from Mentone, the Italian resort, says that as she walked along the street her eyes were arrested by the placard of a newspaper office, headed 'The Johns Hopkins University,' and as she read she discovered what a gift had been made to medical science."[31] Once again the Bryn Mawr School founders were raising standards of education, this time on an even larger world stage. The medical school opened as planned in October of 1893.[32]

Mary Garrett now turned her attention to securing the vacant presidency of Bryn Mawr College for M. Carey Thomas, to ensure that their accomplishments at the fledgling women's college would not be altered. She offered to give $10,000, to be spent at Thomas' discretion, for each year that Thomas served as president. Just as the Hopkins board had hesitated to become indebted to Mary Garrett's terms, the board of Bryn Mawr College was reluctant to place so much power into the hands of a president and her patron. The sum offered represented fully ten percent of the operating budget of the young college, however, and the board accepted, losing two trustees who resigned in disapproval. In 1896, Mary Garrett spent $100,000 renovating and refurnishing the Deanery into a home fit for a college president, a home she would share with Thomas from 1904 to 1915. Additional Garrett money amounting to $400,000 over the ensuing years funded European fellowships, college scholarships, artwork for buildings, books for the library, lectures, and archaeological digs.[33]

By 1896, in the twelve years since she had inherited her money, Mary Garrett had used her funds to directly change the education of women in America, from preschool through the doctoral level, and elevated the national standard for medical training to include women. Her tenacity and business acumen coupled with M. Carey Thomas' sheer determination and academic qualifications made them a formidable force.

The school library

Edith Hamilton

Chapter Two

DELIGHTS OF THE MIND 1896–1922

Class of 1908

*I*n the first years of the school, the members of the board of managers were living at Bryn Mawr College or in frequent travel. Much of the general oversight of the school's affairs fell to Mary Elizabeth Garrett, who was most often in Baltimore, was the most adept at financial matters, and was financing the endeavor herself. Nearly all decisions were agreed upon by the founders, including the admission of students, hiring and firing of faculty, and the awarding of tuition grants. These and more mundane matters were discussed in notes written in the margins of letters that circulated often, sometimes daily, among the women. The volume of mail and telegrams extant today provide evidence of the attention to detail and of the control that the founders maintained in the early years of the school.

Bryn Mawr did not have a headmistress between 1885 and 1896. Instead, the founders placed a series of highly educated "secretaries" in charge of the daily supervision of the school, but left few matters to their sole discretion.[1] The first secretary, Miss Eleanor A. Andrews, who had studied at Newnham College, Cambridge, England, was replaced in 1889 by Mrs. Mary Noyes Colvin, PhD, University of Zurich. Her successor in 1893 was Miss Mary H. Buckingham, a graduate of the Harvard Annex in 1890 and Newnham College. One year later, Miss Ida Wood, BA and MA from Vassar College, PhD from Bryn Mawr College, and former secretary for women at the University of Pennsylvania, took Miss Buckingham's place and remained for two years.[2]

There was a practical, fortuitous side to this arrangement for the board members. They ultimately bore the responsibility for decisions made about the school, but they did not have to deal directly with the parents who did not fully understand the motivation behind their carefully deliberated policies. As Millicent Carey McIntosh, Class of 1916 and niece of M. Carey Thomas, would recall, "A school which insisted that girls should study Latin, which didn't allow them to drop subjects just because they didn't like them, or because they felt they were too delicate to study them, preferred to have only a secretary who . . . reported to Miss Thomas in Bryn Mawr. She, who was a hundred and twenty-five miles away, was safe from the rage of the parents!"[3] Bryn Mawr challenged the existing beliefs about girls' education and was under the constant watch of a dubious community. Many families that could afford to send their daughters to Bryn Mawr were not yet sure they really wanted to do so.

Despite the misgivings of some families, enrollment in the early years increased steadily. Many students came from wealthy families who could afford to pay the tuition, but the school was too expensive for the daughters of professors at Johns Hopkins, the clergy, and middle-class merchants who believed in the progressive education the school offered. Early on, Francis T. King arranged for tuition assistance for several families from associations and organizations with which he was affiliated.[4] The board of managers realized that they needed to bring in someone who might attract more paying families, as well as effectively implement the ideals they had for the school. In 1896 they hired the school's first headmistress, Edith Hamilton. Included in her contract was an incentive of a bonus payment for any year that the school did not suffer a financial deficit under her leadership.[5]

The Hamilton women, 1907. Edith is in top row, center. Below her are sister Alice, cousin Agnes, and sister Margaret, and her mother Gertrude Pond Hamilton.

Edith Hamilton was born in 1867 of American parents near Dresden, Germany, and raised with her younger sisters and brother in Fort Wayne, Indiana. She and her siblings were taught at home privately, as their parents preferred a classical education to the public school's curriculum, which emphasized math and American history.[6] As a young child, Edith Hamilton began her formal education studying Latin and Greek with her father; she spoke French with her mother and German with the household servants. She memorized classical texts and studied the Bible and theology before following family tradition by enrolling in Miss Porter's School for Young Ladies in Farmington, Connecticut, from 1884 to 1886. The Hamilton sisters loved the school and the friendships they formed there, but at the time Porter's was still a blend between the more scholarly female seminary and the traditional finishing school and did not prepare girls for college entrance. Similar to the Baltimore education Bryn Mawr's founders received at Miss Kummer's School on Mount Vernon Place, Miss Porter's would teach "the 'accomplishments' considered essential for young ladies, but grounding these in a solid mix of English, mathematics, languages, and science."[7] Edith returned home to prepare privately for the Bryn Mawr College entrance exams and entered the college in 1890, earning both her bachelor's and master's degrees in Greek and Latin in 1894. She was a Fellow in Latin of Bryn Mawr College in 1894–1895 and received, as the college's best scholar, the prestigious Mary E. Garrett European Fellowship.[8] She was honored as well to join the board of managers of The Bryn Mawr School and was listed as such in the school catalog for 1895–1896.[9] Edith and her sister Alice, who had graduated from the medical school at the University of Michigan in 1893 and desired further work in pathology laboratories, entered the University of Leipzig, where Edith continued her studies in classics.[10] As many of her classmates were clerics, she was forced to sit "in a chair up on the platform beside the lecturer, facing the audience, so that nobody would be contaminated by contact with her."[11] She was disappointed with the emphasis at Leipzig on obscure grammar "instead of the grandeur and beauty of Aeschylus and Sophocles."[12] The sisters withdrew and entered the University of Munich. Although Edith had planned to pursue her doctorate, her father suffered financial reverses and could no longer support his daughters overseas. Edith had to abandon her doctoral studies and finally accepted the repeated offers of M. Carey Thomas to become the first headmistress of The Bryn Mawr School. In the summer of 1896, the Hamilton women returned to America.

Although a gifted scholar of the classics, Edith Hamilton had never taught nor served as an administrator in a school. Her experience was similar to that of M. Carey Thomas before she arrived at Bryn Mawr College to serve as dean. She later related that as she traveled to Baltimore, she thought, "if I were put in charge of running this train, I could hardly know less how to do it than I know how to run The Bryn Mawr School."[13] She was a brilliant choice, however, as she had an infectious love of learning. The great care she showed her students and their families would endear her to them during the twenty-six years she would lead the school into an era of successful progressive education. She would not, however, have an easy time with the board of managers.

Edith Hamilton recognized what the founders, so dedicated to their original ideals yet distant from the daily routines of the school and the families of the students, could not see. To uphold the high college-preparatory standards that the founders insisted on, the school risked alienating Baltimore families who otherwise might approve of the school. Losing a wealthy, well-connected family in the early years

"As a little girl I used to sit on the stairs and hear the meetings of the Board of Managers, of which [my mother] was chairman . . . and I can remember [M. Carey Thomas'] voice coming up the stairs . . . saying 'Miss Hamilton . . . do not let these soft, Baltimore mothers take their daughters out of Latin!'"

Millicent Carey McIntosh, address at Bryn Mawr College upon receiving the M. Carey Thomas Award in 1977

could also mean losing the families of their friends and relatives. By 1910, such girls' schools in the area as Garrison Forest, Girls' Latin, and Roland Park Country could accommodate the demands of these families as they offered a choice between college preparation and a general program. Edith Hamilton understood that the school's future success in Baltimore would depend on satisfying the families that could afford the tuition, as well as those who desired Bryn Mawr's rigorous academics but did not have the means to pay. Edith's constant requests for financial assistance for families placed a greater burden on Mary Elizabeth Garrett, who covered the deficits of the school each year. While M. Carey Thomas could take a firm stance about unpaid bills at the college, which drew students from across the nation, the school had to depend on a much smaller group of families in the city of Baltimore and needed to be more tolerant of those who were late in their payments. In correspondence from 1915 to 1920, Edith argued with her repeatedly over this point.[14]

For the girls of Bryn Mawr, Edith Hamilton personified the educated "New Woman" of the twentieth century. She was elegant, firm but fair, and extremely intellectual. The girls adored being in class with her, and they were unhappy when she was away. They realized that during morning prayers in the silent study hall, she was not reading from the Bible but was reciting passages from memory. Millicent Carey McIntosh recalled, "[one] passage which was her favorite, it seems to me, sums up what was really the essence of the school; it carried us through the difficult work that we had to do, and made us determined to go forward with knowledge, to take ourselves to college even when it was unpopular to go. 'Whatsoever things are good, whatsoever things are true, whatsoever things are lovely, whatsoever things are of good report, if there be any virtue, if there be any knowledge . . . think on these things.'"[15]

Edith Hamilton often lost track of time, and it was considered a privilege to be assigned to find her in the massive school building and bring her to class. "She would slide in, always late, borrow the nearest Cicero or Virgil, settle back in a low chair, dangling a pump on a white toed stocking, and attend with preoccupied patience to our painful renderings, or drop with random repetition those well-remembered items of information–that in Antioch the Christians were called so, the names of the three Greek tragedians . . . Or bending between thumb and finger the card of a waiting visitor, she would pause to emphasize a verse."[16] She sat on the stairs for individual weekly sessions with all the students in the school to go over their grades and reports and see where they needed to work harder. "Even though she was so

". . . she brought in with her the air of having come from some high centre of civilization, where the skies were loftier, the views more spacious, the atmosphere more free and open than with us . . . . One hesitates to use so canting a word, but a real culture was the blessing she made accessible to our young, provincial minds, the familiar commerce with ideas, the liberal pleasures of the intellect . . . . What had sunk so deep in her thoughts carried a reality into ours, and helped us to mean . . . to make some noble profit of our lives."

Grace Branham, 1931 Bryn Mawrtyr

great and so distant in many ways, she could say just the right thing to make us want to do more or better than we were doing. When she taught us she became alive in a way that I could never describe."[17] She was in complete agreement with the board's desire to send as many Baltimore girls to college as possible, and she prepared the girls to challenge themselves and not be afraid of failure. "My own experience . . . made me convinced that the Bryn Mawr College entrance examinations could be passed by every girl who was willing to work hard, very hard in some cases, I admit."[18] The work, however, needed to be meaningful. "But it is not hard work which is dreary; it is superficial work. That is always boring in the long run, and it has always seemed strange to me that in our endless discussions about education so little stress is ever laid on the pleasure of becoming an educated person, the enormous interest it adds to life."[19]

The school continued to attract highly educated teachers of that first generation of women who were able to choose a career in teaching college-preparatory classes. Some were quite intimidating to the young Bryn Mawr students. Anne Kinsolving Brown, Class of 1924, remembered that the ones who truly connected with students "always managed to convince us that the ultimate purpose of work was pleasure, and that solid accomplishment could be rapturous. They conducted their classes as if they were determined to admit us to the forest, and never mind the trees."[20]

Not surprisingly, many of the teachers were actively involved in the suffrage movement and attended gatherings and meetings in Baltimore, Annapolis, and Washington, D.C. Edith Hamilton and the school physician Dr. Mary Sherwood were often speakers at suffrage meetings organized by Bryn Mawr School founders Bessie King Ellicott and Julia Rogers, who had drafted legislation in 1911 and 1912, respectively, for municipal suffrage for the women of Baltimore.[21] At Bryn Mawr, a Junior Suffrage League was formed to provide speakers on issues that the girls would then discuss and debate.

Bryn Mawr began a Primary Division in 1894, as families with daughters enrolled in the school requested accommodation for their younger daughters as well. Margaret Hamilton, Edith's sister, came to Bryn Mawr to teach science in 1901, after she had received her degree in chemistry and biology in 1897 from Bryn Mawr College and had studied abroad on the Mary E. Garrett European Fellowship. In

"I was a lover of the Greeks when I came to Baltimore, and they helped me with the school. You see, whenever a number of people come together there is always the basic problem of the claims of the individual and the claims of the community. I had to get every girl in school, if I could, to feel her own responsibility for the school."

Edith Hamilton, 1958–1959

Mary Snowden, Bryn Mawr playground teacher, 1924-1963, reading to students

1910 she became the director of the Primary Division and spent thirty-four years at the school, serving several times as interim headmistress. The Hamilton sisters realized that although the Primary Division relied financially on the coffers of the Main School, it provided a steady stream of students prepared for the Main School. At the same time, it satisfied the needs of the school's families and strengthened the relationships between them. The women lobbied for several years to set up "baby classes" in primary schools in other locations at the perimeter of the city to prepare children to continue their educations on the main campus. The board of managers did not agree, however, and the plan was never put into action. By 1909, Bryn Mawr had a waiting list for the Main School, and in 1920 a building next door at 1200 Cathedral Street was purchased to house the growing Primary. Margaret Hamilton began to admit boys to the primary grades in the autumn of 1926 at the request of families. By the spring of 1944, their last year on campus, more than eighty boys had attended The Bryn Mawr School for Girls of Baltimore City in their early years.

Edith Hamilton also recognized that Bryn Mawr School students who did not go on to college often had a desire to put their skills and abilities to work in service to the Baltimore community. In 1910 she created the Bryn Mawr School League as a

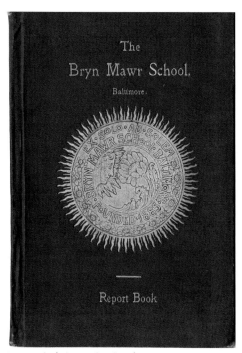

Report Book of Clare Hardy, Class of 1922

community service organization for alumnae, who would operate a branch of the Baltimore Young Women's Christian Association at 1224 Light Street. In addition to offering young working women room and board, alumnae provided instruction in a variety of such practical skills as sewing, hat making, and clerical work, as well as classes in literature, health, and physical education. In the summer, the league hosted women at the seashore and on ferry trips to Annapolis and the Chesapeake Bay. They tutored children, held Bible classes, and taught women and young children Bryn Mawr's favorite sport of basketball. Much of this was funded by donations, but league women also hosted a variety of fund-raising events that included plays and athletics, which were advertised in *The Baltimore Sun.* Their work was chronicled in the *Bryn Mawrtyr*, and students in the school often contributed to the league's fund-raising efforts. Hundreds of women, many seeking to make their way alone in the city, and immigrants with no local connections, survived their first years in Baltimore thanks to the work of these dedicated alumnae of The Bryn Mawr School.[22]

In a letter to M. Carey Thomas, Edith Hamilton described the first Alumnae Day that she had decided to hold at the school on March 27, 1913.[23] She invited alumnae to the school to visit classes, to have lunch with the seniors, and to attend "a little private Gymnastic Exhibition." She would then dismiss the school at one thirty in the afternoon to allow for a basketball game between alumnae and students. She acknowledged that, "I have realized in the last two years as never before, how very valuable to the school a strong Alumnae Association would be and I want now to try to bring the girls into direct relation with the school for one day every year."[24] In 1915, the Alumnae Association was given the right to elect members to the board. As alumnae began in earnest to raise funds for an endowment, Edith Hamilton urged M. Carey Thomas in 1920 that "a board with larger representation from Baltimore" was needed, as the people of Baltimore now "will support a college-preparatory school for girls" and would desire a voice in its direction.[25]

The first Bryn Mawr uniform was instituted by Edith Hamilton in 1914, after the fashion of those worn in England. The winter version was of dark blue wool serge, with a full-gored skirt and a tunic with a handkerchief pocket. The lighter summer version was of Peter Thompson linen. An unidentified newspaper article entitled "Uniform at Bryn Mawr, Girls May No Longer Vie With Each Other In The Matter of Frocks," noted that they had been "specially designed to give the girls a perfectly free and easy movement."[26]

"[The alumnae] have an ideal now before them in working for an endowment to keep in Baltimore a school such as they, themselves, went to, the only kind of a school they believe in, a school not for the rich only, but for the people who cannot afford to pay high tuition fees and for that very reason need more than the others the best possible training for their daughters. They will not work for an endowment for any reason less imperative than this, that unless an endowment is raised the tuition fees must increase, and that any material increase beyond the present fees will result in the school's being beyond the means of all but the rich."

Edith Hamilton, in a letter to M. Carey Thomas, November 23, 1920

Mary Elizabeth Garrett died in April 1915, leaving the bulk of her now much-depleted estate to her lifelong friend, M. Carey Thomas. She believed that Thomas would continue to provide financial support to the causes they had both believed in so deeply, but Garrett made no restrictions upon her to do so. Garrett's will left the building and all its furnishings and equipment to the school, but stipulated that The Bryn Mawr School would "conduct and maintain a school for girls as a college preparatory school exclusively." In the event that the school altered its mission of college preparation, all the assets she had endowed to it would revert to M. Carey Thomas. A codicil, drafted just days before her death, forgave the debt of $55,000 that she had loaned to the school in the years leading up to 1902 in order to keep the school solvent.[27]

The Bryn Mawr School, corner of Cathedral and Preston Streets

A two-story outdoor study hall was erected in the garden during the turn-of-the-century fresh air movement.

Inside, younger girls and their teachers bundled up in coats, as they read with the windows open.

World War I brought greater financial struggles for Bryn Mawr as many fathers were sent overseas to fight. Tuition bills went unpaid, some students were withdrawn, and greater financial assistance was needed to help those who remained. Inflation caused by the war nearly doubled tuition from $250 in 1915 to $400 in 1920, just five years later.

By the beginning of the 1920s, the continual conflicts over finances and school policy between M. Carey Thomas and Edith Hamilton had begun to take a toll on the headmistress' health. Edith Hamilton offered her resignation, but was persuaded to stay on longer. School families and alumnae tried to convince her to remain at the school, but by the spring of 1922 her departure made the national newspapers. It was seen by many as the result of M. Carey Thomas' efforts to push Edith Hamilton out of the school. Newspaper articles speculated that Thomas desired to head The Bryn Mawr School, as she had just retired as president of Bryn Mawr College.

Edith Hamilton had brought the school from its primary function of raising the standard of girls' education in Baltimore and preparing girls for college, to a practical, functioning institution of national renown.[28] Her wisdom, generous spirit, and careful guidance had led the fledgling school to exemplify excellence in girls' education that would benefit women for generations. Upon her retirement, alumnae commissioned the noted artist Lydia Field Emmet to paint her portrait. It is the only portrait that Edith Hamilton ever sat for, and today it hangs in the entrance to the Edith Hamilton Library at The Bryn Mawr School.[29]

Edith Hamilton, by Lydia Field Emmet, 1925

The Bryn Mawr School campus at the time of purchase, 1928

Chapter Three

THE MOVE TO THE COUNTRY 1922–1939

First staff of The Quill, 1923

*T*he school board chose Amy Kelly, a professor of English at Wellesley College, to succeed Edith Hamilton in May 1922. She recently had prepared an acclaimed study of secondary girls' schools and women's colleges, and her recommendations for "some radical changes in the traditional subject matter and methods" would become the basis for the founding of Bennington College in Vermont.[1] The Bryn Mawr School board felt that she would lead the school into a new era. In 1922, Amy Kelly became the second headmistress of Bryn Mawr in thirty-seven years.

Over the years more Baltimore girls were choosing to attend women's colleges other than Bryn Mawr. The requirement to pass the Bryn Mawr College entrance examinations to graduate from The Bryn Mawr School meant that many of those students had to prepare for Bryn Mawr's exams, as well as the exams for another college or those of the College Board. The emphasis on languages and certain aspects of the sciences at Bryn Mawr College differed enough from that of other colleges that it greatly complicated planning the school's curriculum. Often teachers were required to tutor students for elements of the different college exams privately. As Amy Kelly explained to the board on January 10, 1925, "Girls preparing for Vassar will certainly go to another school rather than face the almost impossible difficulty of meeting both requirements. This would seem to me to suggest to the public, which does not understand the technicalities involved, that we cannot prepare girls for Vassar in The Bryn Mawr School."[2] Parents urged the school to prepare students instead for the exams of the national College Entrance Examination Board, which Bryn Mawr College had begun to accept soon after 1900.[3] Bound by both tradition and the charter of the school, Bryn Mawr continued to require the college's exam for graduation until 1927, when the college finally abandoned its own entrance exams.

By 1928, three hundred fifty students were crowded into the Main and Primary school buildings, and the existing playgrounds, athletic fields, and gymnasium space were inadequate. The fields were not regulation size for hockey or lacrosse, and those available for rent were inconvenient and unsatisfactory. Mary Elizabeth Garrett's Montebello property, with its dense woods and uneven terrain, proved to be too far away and too expensive to develop properly to use for athletics on a regular basis. The area around the school buildings was becoming increasingly congested and polluted, and the streets now served as thoroughfares for commercial traffic and parades. Families were beginning to move north out of downtown Baltimore to live in the country settings of Homeland, Guilford, and Roland Park, and some schools were following them. The Country School, soon renamed for board member Daniel Coit Gilman, moved in 1910 from its original Homewood House campus on the new grounds of Johns Hopkins University, to its present site on Roland Avenue.[4] Girls' Latin, which had separated from Goucher College in 1909, moved in 1927 from Winans Mansion on St. Paul Street to its last home at 10 Club Road in Roland Park.[5] Friends School purchased land for its current campus on Charles Street in 1925, leaving its own large city schoolhouse on Park Avenue by 1936.[6] Bryn Mawr was under increasing pressure from parents to move out of Mary Elizabeth Garrett's magnificent, but now crowded and aging building at Cathedral and Preston Streets, and establish a country setting for their daughters nearer their new suburban homes.

The
Bryn Mawr School

*A Frank, Business-Like Statement
of its
Financial Need for
$300,000*

Building to be Occupied
in September
by Primary School

Solicitor enter here
amount paid, if any

Received from

Name

Address

Print Name and Address of Subscriber Above 1928

In consideration of the subscription of others and for the purpose of purchasing and developing a country site for THE BRYN MAWR SCHOOL, and to create an Endowment to insure its future, I hereby subscribe

.....................($) Dollars,

payable every six months, beginning June 1st, 1928, and ending June 1st, 1931, or as follows:

Check $ ....

Cash $ ....

Do not write in space below

Date	Payment	Balance

Total Subscription

Cash herewith

Or payable................

$................

$................

$................

$................

$................

$................

Signature ....

Address ....

Make checks payable to Bryn Mawr School Fund

Solicitor ....

**Make checks payable to
BRYN MAWR SCHOOL FUND
Preston & Cathedral Sts., Baltimore, Md.**

Brochure and subscription card for the 1928 building campaign

M. Carey Thomas opposed such a move as a potential conflict to Mary Garrett's wishes for the school and her will, until she received assurance that there was no plan to alter the school's academic focus by moving to the country. On March 9, 1928, *The Baltimore Sun* announced that Bryn Mawr would purchase twenty-six acres of the Douglas H. Gordon estate known as The Orchards. The school would establish a campaign to raise $200,000 to purchase and renovate the existing property, and an additional $100,000, to settle a provision of debt released by M. Carey Thomas, to establish an endowment for the school.[7] Committees were formed to oversee the planning of buildings and the complex financial considerations involved in purchasing and developing the property, as well as disposing of the current school buildings. For the first time, men were asked to take part in the decision-making process of the school's activities. The Men's Advisory Committee on Financial Policy, consisting of six businessmen familiar with real estate, taxes, and investments, advised that no considerable financial undertaking begin until the Cathedral Street school buildings were sold. A Committee of Nine included representatives of the board of managers, the Alumnae Association, and the school staff to consider the site layout and building plans. Both of these committees reported to the executive boards of the Alumnae and Parents' Associations, in consultation with the board of managers.[8] This was a marked step away from the proprietary school that had been run by the founders, and a move toward a more inclusive decision-making process by those who had a close relationship with the school and who represented the school's past, present, and future.

The campaign, which ran from May 1–18, 1928, netted $100,000 in donations from alumnae, faculty, and parents.[9] The board chose to make a $50,000 down payment on the property and take a $100,000 mortgage to finance the balance of the purchase. The remaining $50,000 was matched by a loan taken on the Cathedral Street building to make the necessary improvements to the new school property. This would allow the school to begin the much-needed move onto the new campus, but left no money for the anticipated endowment fund. There was no prospective buyer for the Cathedral Street buildings.

The Gordon Building, 1928

Margaret Hamilton moved the Primary School and Main I (grade five) into the renovated Gordon house in September 1928. This move allowed the school to rent out the Primary building downtown, while a master plan was developed for the new campus. Donations from alumnae to provide classroom quarters as well as some limited space for the Athletics Department permitted the renovation of the dilapidated Gate House in 1929. The school was able to announce in the *The Sun* that all afternoon activities of the one hundred eighty students in the Main School would be held on the new campus beginning September 1930.[10]

M. Carey Thomas, by then an advocate of the move, believed the new school should resemble the architectural style of the University of Virginia, with a group of neo-classical brick buildings surrounding a common area. In 1931, as the first component of this plan, the Mary Elizabeth Garrett Building was constructed not

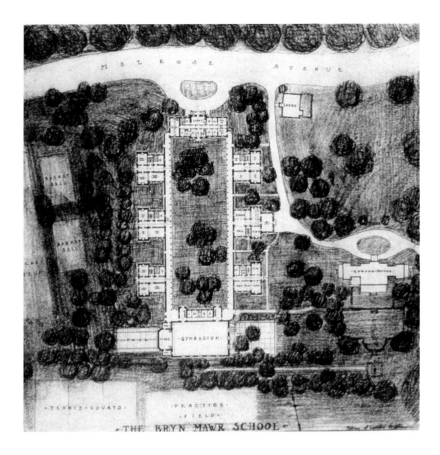

of brick but of stone from the Butler Quarry to match the eighteenth-century Gate House on the property. Mains II and III (grades six and seven) moved into the new Garrett Building in the fall of 1931, and fields were finally ready for athletic use. For the first time, all Bryn Mawr athletic teams could play at the school. The older girls now spent the morning in class at the Cathedral Street building and would then go to the new campus in the afternoon for study hall and athletics. The Garrett Building's cost of nearly $50,000 had been funded by the sale of a playground lot on Brevard Street next to the main building downtown, residues from the campaign, and from borrowed money.[11] The school had now depleted all of its credit, and there was no more money available to borrow. The *Alumnae Bulletin* warned that "future building of the other units [would] depend entirely on new gifts or the sale of the town property."[12]

Student Government in 1935. President Edith Hooker, Vice President Mary Brown Klinefelter and class representatives M. Streeter, J. Miles, N. Cadwalader, A.L. Thomas, and M. Ridgely. The uniform continues to be a dark and light blue.

Amy Kelly was granted a year's absence from 1932–1933 to continue her research on the medieval queen, Eleanor of Aquitaine. Her book, published by Harvard in 1950, would become a seminal biography of the queen. On her return from Europe in the spring of 1933, she chose to resign and returned to Wellesley. Margaret Hamilton and Elizabeth Thomas had been running the school in her absence, and Margaret Hamilton would continue to oversee the school as interim headmistress until 1935. The effects of the Depression were at their gravest throughout 1933, with few reserves left for either institutions or the individuals who depended upon them. Bank accounts were closed, loans were called, and salaries were drastically cut. Bryn Mawr could not meet payroll consistently, and like many other businesses, requested its employees to take a reduction in pay. By June of 1933, faculty and staff were owed more than $8,000, and in 1935 agreed to disregard half the debt still owed to them as a contribution to the school's future. Several years passed before the dedicated faculty of Bryn Mawr could stabilize their own finances, but they were driven by their concern for the future of the school and their dedication to their students.

By the spring of 1933, Bryn Mawr could no longer afford to continue operating on two campuses, and on June 3 *The Baltimore Sun* announced that the school had purchased a prefabricated building from the Episcopal Cathedral of the Incarnation and would move it to the Melrose campus, where it would serve as the study hall and library.[13] Margaret Hamilton reported to the alumnae that they accomplished the move by dividing larger classrooms into smaller ones, adding two new rooms to the back of the study hall, and building a temporary gymnasium, which was "so completely satisfactory both in size, lighting and looks, that it will be a possession for always. It serves also for the plays, the size is larger than the town gymnasium and the acoustics better."[14] This temporary building is today's "Old Gym." The senior class had lost its beloved Senior Room, and the Athletic Department still needed offices and locker rooms; but finally, the entire school would reside on the Melrose campus.

The Cathedral Street building was closed, awaiting a buyer. Without students in the building, the furnaces weren't fired and moisture on the walls began to damage the artwork and plaster casts for which there was no room on the new campus. By 1935, what had not been sold or given away was put in storage. Two years later, the Garrison Forest School bought a large bas-relief of Amazonians. In 1938, Bryn Mawr loaned the Parthenon frieze to the Roland Park Country School for ten years, and in October of 1947 accepted the offer of $300 by the school's alumnae board to purchase what remained of it after a fire that summer damaged all but the library and a secondary gymnasium.[15] Another fire just two weeks later destroyed much of the Boys' Latin School near the former Bryn Mawr building at Cathedral Street, prompting Bryn Mawr and other Baltimore institutions to reevaluate their insurance policies.[16]

In many ways, 1935, the 50th anniversary of The Bryn Mawr School, was a pivotal year for the institution. With the entire school finally unified on the new country campus in a beautiful and open setting, morning classes could be followed by afternoon study, athletics, and a variety of activities. It also marked the end of the city school era. Margaret Hamilton, who had served the school since 1901, had told the board in 1933 when she agreed to become acting headmistress that she would retire within two years and did so. A lovely crayon portrait of her by noted Boston artist Lillian Westcott Hale was presented to the school the following fall at the annual meeting of the Parents' Association. Dr. Mary Sherwood, school physician since 1894, whose responsible care of the students had brought accolades from the city as well as from other schools, died in May 1935. And M. Carey Thomas, who had resigned from the board in the spring of 1928 and spent much of her time in extensive travel, died on December 2, 1935. The departure of these three women, administrators of the school from its earliest days, marked the passing of the school from an innovative urban institution of the nineteenth century to a progressive leader of girls' education in the twentieth.

Margaret Hamilton, crayon sketch by Lillian Westcott Hale

Dr. Janet Howell Clark

The board chose Dr. Janet Howell Clark, Class of 1906, to become the next headmistress. Dr. Clark had graduated from Bryn Mawr College in 1910 and in 1913 received her doctoral degree in physics from Johns Hopkins, after which she taught at Bryn Mawr and Smith Colleges. Dr. Clark, an expert in biophysics and ultraviolet radiation, had been with the School of Hygiene and Public Health at Hopkins for many years when she agreed to lead Bryn Mawr. Her husband, Dr. Admont H. Clark had died in the influenza epidemic in 1918, and their daughter, Anne Janet Clark, was in the senior class of 1935 at the school.

The focus of the next several years was trying to balance finances: paying down debt; raising salaries; trying to sell the Cathedral Street property to take out building loans for the new campus; quietly raising money without starting another formal campaign; and carefully building essential minor structures to meet the needs of the more than three hundred students on the campus. The board repeatedly considered the construction of the next substantial building, already calling it "Hamilton," but was bound by existing debt and could not borrow the money necessary to build it. The Gordon drive was shifted from the west to the east side of the Gate House in the summer of 1936 to protect children from cars going up to the Primary, and a locker room was added to the west end of the gymnasium, permitting the lower rooms in the Gate House to be turned into much-needed classrooms.

The city eventually assessed property taxes on the Cathedral Street assets, as they were no longer being used as a school, prompting the board to consider demolishing the building to eliminate the tax liability. The board was so eager to sell off the building that it offered a reward of $1,800 to any alumna who found a buyer.[17]

Class	VIII²*	VII²	VI²	V³	IV³	III³	II³
English	5†	4	4	4	4	4	5
Mathematics	4	4	3 (C division 4)	4	4	4	4
Latin	4	4 Alternate choice: Greek.	4	4	4	4	..
Greek	..	4	4 Alternate choice: German, Science or History.	....	3 Alternate choice: German or Science.	..	..
French	..	4 (B division 5)	4	4	3 (C division 4)	3	4
German	..	....	Alternate choice: Greek, Science or History.	Alternate choice: Greek.	3 Alternate choice: Greek or Science.	..	..
Science	6	....	3 Alternate choice: Greek, German or History.	....	3 Alternate choice: Greek or German.	..	2
History	..	5 Ancient	American 3 Alternate choice: Greek, German or Science.	English 4 Alternate choice: Greek or German.	....	4	4
Music	..	....	....	....	1	1	1
Drawing	..	....	....	....	1	1	1
Gymnasium	2	2	2	2	2	2	2
Assembly	1	1	1	1	1	1	1
No. periods per week.	22	24	21	23	23	24	24
No. study periods.	8	6	9	7	7	6	6
Time required for Home Work: Minimum average per lesson.	1 hour	45 min.	45 min.	40 min.	40 min.	30 min.	30 min.

*Small Arabic numerals indicate the number of divisions of the class.
†Large Arabic numerals indicate the number of periods of recitation per week.

1930–1931 curriculum

In the summer of 1937, an addition to the north side of Garrett costing close to $12,000 was built to provide a teachers' room and new offices for the administration, freeing former office space to become a small library.

According to the Alumnae Bulletin, the Primary also needed more room to support its "very unusual training in music and drawing and also regular gymnasium and dancing classes in which emphasis is laid on posture and rhythmic movement."[18] Interest in handicraft work for the younger girls grew so much that an addition was made to the music building for a workshop, where two afternoons a week the younger students learned "basketry, carpentry, wood-carving, pottery, weaving on looms, metal work, making clothes and hooked rugs."[19]

Finally, in May of 1938, after several years of lengthy negotiations with a variety of interested parties, Dr. Clark could announce to the alumnae that the Deutsches Haus, an incorporation of more than sixty disparate German singing societies, had rented the Cathedral Street school building with an option to buy the property. They also were prepared to clean and renovate the building and install a new heating system.[20] Although Bryn Mawr would ultimately be responsible for the mortgage on the property if the rent were not paid, this was a great relief.

Dr. Clark informed the board the next month that she had been offered the position of professor of biology and dean of the College for Women at the University of Rochester. Her contract bound her to Bryn Mawr until April 1939, but she was

The Bryn Mawr School campus, 1933

needed in Rochester by January, if possible. Recognizing the outstanding opportunity offered to Dr. Clark, the board reluctantly accepted her resignation, formed a search committee to find the next headmistress, and once again asked Elizabeth Thomas to lead the school during the interim.

In the meantime, tardy tuition payments combined with a dramatic decline in enrollment in the Primary created an alarming situation as another year of greater deficit became probable. While the Main School had only three fewer registrations than the current year, there were twenty-one fewer contracts for the Primary School. The Depression years were still taking their toll as a nationwide decline in births led to forty percent fewer children between the ages of one and eight. Enrollment, which had peaked at one hundred eighty-five students at Bryn Mawr in the Primary in 1931–1932, was reduced to only eighty-four students for the 1939–1940 school year.

When the search committee presented Katharine Van Bibber as its top choice for headmistress from a field of seven finalists, the board quickly agreed that she was the ideal candidate for the school. An alumna from the Class of 1920 and winner of the Bryn Mawr College scholarship, Van Bibber had majored in math, physics, and chemistry before returning to teach algebra and physics at The Bryn Mawr School from 1924 to 1926. She then used the Bryn Mawr College European Scholarship that she had been awarded in 1924 to study chemistry for a year at University College, London. On her return she taught briefly at Rosemary Hall in Connecticut before going to New York's Brearley School, where she headed the math department, and in 1934 became the assistant to headmistress Millicent Carey McIntosh. She earned her master's degree in mathematics at Columbia University and had begun work there toward her doctorate.[21]

Members of the Class of 1951 visit the United Nations

Chapter Four

THE BRYN MAWR SCHOOL NEVER CLOSES 1939–1962

Members of the Class of 1948 planting a tree in Main II, 1940-1941

Katharine Van Bibber requested that three issues be addressed before she agreed to accept the offer of The Bryn Mawr School board: that the older faculty have their salaries raised before any more money would be used for buildings; that a faculty member be added to the board of managers; and that the Primary School be reorganized. The board, which had been considering each of these issues, was ready to comply. In fact, Dr. Clark already had alerted the Primary School faculty that there would be layoffs as the result of the drop in enrollment. Dr. Clark left for the University of Rochester in January of 1939, and Elizabeth Thomas oversaw the school until Miss Van Bibber's arrival in the summer.

Although the Bryn Mawr College entrance examinations had not been used since 1927, Miss Van Bibber found that the school curriculum continued to center on preparing students for them. Latin was still required of all students through senior year, a requirement which she felt was an unnecessary burden for those who didn't enjoy it. She changed the rules so that seniors could take "English, Physics, and . . . History, and one of the following: Latin, French, Mathematics or Bible." Katharine Van Bibber wrote that "the Latin department never forgave her."[1] In the summer of 1940, colleges informed Bryn Mawr and other preparatory schools that they would no longer provide them with feedback on how their students were doing in the college curriculum. Previously, the schools had received transcripts and often written commentary on their graduates' progress, which teachers had used to evaluate how well they were preparing their students and to alert them to shifts in college coursework. The Bryn Mawr School's relationship with the college had been essential from the beginning and had directly determined the curriculum over the years. In the case of history, Edith Hamilton recounted that she "fought a battle-royal with the History Department of Bryn Mawr College because they wanted me to drop all history from the school. Don't send us any girls, they said, with silly stories in their heads about Alfred and the cakes, or George Washington and his little hatchet. We can teach them much better if you just leave it all to us."[2] She was dismayed over a "Greek entrance examination where my girls who had learned their Greek as Bryn Mawr College told them to, by reading Xenophon's *March of the 10,000* and the *Iliad*'s battles of god and men on the ringing plains of windy Troy, were made to turn into Greek one of Aesop's fables about a frog."[3]

Presentations by college representatives in the early 1940s at school assemblies reflected the girls' desires not to be too isolated from men by going to women's colleges. The dean of Radcliffe College told the students that they "should consider going to college very seriously before making a decision, and gave [them] a new line on co-educational college, where she told [them], 'One lives from date to date.'" In February of 1940, the Mount Holyoke representative noted that the frequent visits of men from nearby Amherst, as well as the dramatic productions they presented together gave the campus an "almost co-educational" feel. In the 1940s, most Bryn Mawr School graduates continued to enroll at the women's colleges, with the occasional girl choosing instead a coeducational environment such as Bucknell, Swarthmore, or the University of Michigan.

As headmistress, Katharine Van Bibber had an interesting perspective on Bryn Mawr's development from her years as a student in the first decade of the twentieth century under Edith Hamilton, and as a teacher in the 1920s with Amy Kelly. "When I was a BMS student, no one had ever thought that a school curriculum should be 'relevant' to life. The Roman history, the classic myths, and the elementary algebra taught in the seventh grade were pure delight. We did not care whether they would be useful or not; they were fun. The same was true of eighteenth-century essays in the tenth grade and nineteenth-century English novels in the eleventh, and of course, Vergil with Miss Hamilton in the senior class."[4] She would later write to the school community about Bryn Mawr in the 1940s, that "while we were broadening our interests in extra-curricular activities, we kept our minds fixed on the ultimate goals of education: rational thinking, tolerance, compassion, all of which are to be found in an active imagination and a critical ability to detect fallacies. A necessary condition for achieving these goals is, I am convinced, that the process be fun."[5]

Katharine Van Bibber

The mortgage held by the trustees of the Gordon estate on the school property did not have a finite term and was chronically overdue as the school could not always meet the scheduled payment. In 1940, larger payments were required in order to continue with the mortgage, adding another $2,500 to the cost each year. The mortgage was called in October of 1941 and had to be paid in full within ninety days. Johns Hopkins Hospital agreed to hold a $75,000 mortgage for a term of five years, asking that the school spend $5,000 in repairs on the buildings, and that they raise $10,000 to meet the Gordon obligations.

*Katharine Van Bibber with alumnae faculty and staff,
1958–1959*

Katharine Van Bibber was delighted with the Bryn Mawr that she returned to in 1939. She found that "the best faculty it has ever been my good fortune to encounter in a secondary school" combined with the "sense of responsibility and a maturity of purpose" demonstrated by the upper classes made Bryn Mawr truly unique among schools. "Throughout the school, from the Kindergarten to Class VIII (twelfth grade), day after day, and week after week, in every class, the Bryn Mawr girls meet with enthusiasm and imagination of the true scholar and when necessary, the patience and thoroughness of the expert teacher."[6] The individual attention and guidance that the teachers provided and the eagerness and desire of the students to challenge themselves with the required work made an ideal educational setting for both. She found that the older girls were capable and mature enough to take on tasks and follow through with them quite independently of adult supervision, allowing them to thrive not only academically but in all their pursuits on campus. Student publications, stage settings, fund-raising events, and club activities were well thought-out and administered by the girls, providing an example for the younger classes. Katharine Van Bibber attributed this to the fact that the curriculum taught them to think, but also that "they learn . . . to govern their own lives by reason and experience, and to make themselves effective and well-ordered individuals."[7]

Changes in educational theory and a world at war led Bryn Mawr and other schools to loosen the strictly regimented progression through academic subjects and to allow more flexibility in coursework. At Bryn Mawr the students began to explore subjects that were meaningful to them while still adhering to the classical core of humanistic education of the founders and Edith Hamilton. Language, literature, math, sciences, and history could be taught with greater emphasis on the ideas rather than limited to conscripted facts, "required word-lists, or prescribed theorems." "We do not regard the acquisition of information as important for its own sake, but we do think that training in the intelligent use of information is an essential part of education," reported Miss Van Bibber to the alumnae.[8] The curriculum provided a structure within which current events of the war-torn world could be examined and understood, and more frequent outside speakers brought different points of view to the school community.

"On the eighth of December, the day after Pearl Harbor, The Bryn Mawr School, excused from classes, sat on the floor of the gymnasium in utter silence to hear the [radio broadcast of] the President asking Congress to declare war on Japan. At the end of the speech, the School rose with solemn faces for the 'Star Spangled Banner,' and then filed, still silent, back to its lessons."[9] Many Bryn Mawr families were affected directly by World War II as fathers and brothers went off to war and mothers and sisters took support positions at such places as the Bendix plant in Baltimore, or volunteered in numerous war effort endeavors. By March of 1942, with restrictions on rubber for tires and gas for cars, Katharine Van Bibber was concerned that the thirty families in the Ruxton area would have to withdraw in the fall, and she sought alternative transportation with bus companies and trains. School trips were curtailed, and it became difficult for families to come to school events. Tuition would have to be increased to cover the additional operating costs that the school was incurring, and several part-time teachers had to be let go. The faculty was given a seven-and-a-half percent salary increase to keep up with the greater cost of living expenses because of the war.

Primary classroom on the second floor of Gordon, 1945

In 1942, Harvard, Princeton, and Yale were followed quickly by other American colleges to shift to a wartime twelve-month academic calendar to accept freshmen in May and admit them in June, in order to shorten their time in college to three years and send them on to officers' training. The College Entrance Examination Board had developed the Scholastic Aptitude Test (SAT) as an alternative to the traditional essay exams in 1926, to "test intellectual ability without excessive reliance on any specific subject matter."[10] The test had proved much less popular with both applicants and institutions. This SAT, however, was taken in April, whereas the traditional essay exams were held in June, too late for the new admissions cycle. The men's colleges shifted to the earlier exam, and many of the women's colleges did so as well, as the decrease in numbers would skew the statistics for coeducational institutions. The abrupt drop in registration led the College Board to cancel the June exam, thus ending essay examinations for American college admissions and the need for schools to prepare specifically for them. This would allow for even more stretching of high-school curricula. Students who felt particularly well prepared could take achievement tests in individual subjects, but this would now be a matter of preference rather than a requirement. As Miss Van Bibber commented, "There is now to be greater freedom for teacher and pupils within the limits of the several subjects.

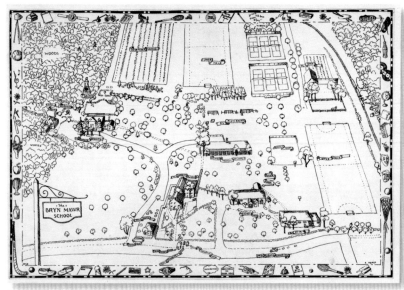

Campus map, 1950, by Elsie Kemp, Class of 1950

This by-product of the war is a welcome one, for we believe that it will give us an opportunity for more constructive education."[11] The entire senior class at Bryn Mawr did well enough on the "experimental" test to merit a handshake at commencement, and the faculty voted that any girl who failed her final school exams would be given another chance the week after commencement.

The war also brought a heightened sense of national duty and a greater desire to promote citizenship and ethics in schools. Dean Richard M. Gummere of Harvard and Headmaster Claude M. Fuess of Andover had written in the May 1942 *Atlantic*

Monthly of necessary changes in the curriculum at boys' private schools beyond military training and other technical skills. As Dr. Gummere stated, "They are striving to carry out the purpose which Georges Duhamel has called 'the closing of the tragic gap between thinking and doing'. . . to equip boys and girls with a culture which both Matthew Arnold and Thomas A. Edison would appreciate." New courses added in the next few years at Bryn Mawr would include an economics class, in which the students would learn about "money and credit, and the pitfalls to be found in both monopolistic and government planning," art history and appreciation, and a Bible class in the development of religious thought.[12]

Mains VII and VIII were learning first aid in an afternoon class once a week and were on equal footing with the teachers, who joined them as students. *Quill* editorials urged seniors to go to college, as the country needed them to finish their education and to take jobs in the summer to support the war effort. "We go to school all winter, and educating ourselves to live as responsible citizens in a democracy has been accepted at present as our main job, and so the only time we have to do something really immediately constructive for the war effort is the summer." Girls were encouraged to help in "a defense factory turning out the desperately needed war materials," or in one of Baltimore's many canneries, preparing fresh food to send overseas. They could volunteer in hospitals and for civil defense, and even young girls could help out on farms that had lost workers to the war effort. *The Quill* listed everyone in the school who had a father, brother, or mother in the services. Bryn Mawr joined the Inter-High School Congress, an organization to "improve and further the war work now being done by the high schools in the city." Main II sold $13,000 worth of war bonds and stamps, enough to fuel a ship for a trip "all the way around the world at the equator."[13] Several classes put on plays, while another gathered and cut kindling and firewood around campus to sell, all to benefit the Red Cross. The younger girls tended a Victory garden (where the Lower School sits today), while others cleaned the grounds of the school once a week. All the while, noted Katharine Van Bibber, "the School emphasizes accuracy, imagination, resourcefulness and the ability to think clearly" to "train the girls for enlightened and useful citizenship in the world after the war." But while the curriculum had become more flexible, with more course choices available in the last two years, the school could "still hold fast to the ideals that have been inherent in The Bryn Mawr School since its founding."[14]

Once the school could finally raise teachers' salaries to pre-Depression levels, the board determined to institute a pension program. Although Social Security had begun in 1937, employees of nonprofit organizations would not be eligible until 1950 and were completely dependent on private plans. December 8, 1941 had been inauspiciously chosen as the date to kick off a campaign to raise funds, but the invasion of Pearl Harbor caused greater uncertainty about the coming years. Not enough funds could be gathered to meet both the obligations of refinancing the debt and beginning a pension plan. It wasn't until the spring of 1943 that the majority of the younger teachers joined Bryn Mawr's first pension plan. Teachers older than fifty, most of whom already had private funds invested, opted not to join as they were too close to retirement to make it worthwhile. The school set aside $1,000 each year as a fund for older faculty members to draw upon as they retired and brought new faculty into the pension plan each year. Anne Williams Niles, president of the Alumnae Association, urged alumnae to share the news with prospective parents, as "we can now hold up our heads in pride as the only girls' private school in Baltimore which has such a system."[15]

Between 1928, when the school took out the first mortgage on the Cathedral Street holdings to purchase the property in the country, and 1941, "during as critical a time economically as our country had ever known, the School ha[d] not only cut its indebtedness in half, it ha[d] appreciably increased its value by improvements to old buildings, and the erection of several new ones."[16]

In April of 1944, the Deutsches Haus was finally able to purchase the Cathedral Street building from Bryn Mawr for $53,500, but only by assuming the school's mortgage with the Savings Bank of Baltimore. The school underwrote the risk, as no one was willing to give Germans a mortgage at the time. Since the mortgage covered the entire downtown property of the school, when Bryn Mawr sold 1200 Cathedral Street (the former Primary building) in October of 1944, the bank would release it from the mortgage, but held back $12,000 until the Deutsches Haus finished paying it off. This provided Bryn Mawr with an annual revenue of $540 a year in earned interest.

Study Hall, circa 1947

Although there had been concern about school enrollment when Katharine Van Bibber arrived in 1939, and again with the onset of war soon after, 1944 brought the highest enrollment yet, with 206 students in the Main School and 122 students in the Primary. Careful supervision of finances had brought stability, but the school was not free to act as it pleased. The Office of Defense Transportation repeatedly denied the school's appeals to purchase a larger school bus, as the mileage on the existing bus was too low to warrant replacement by wartime standards. The school also had to heed the War Labor Board's ruling of reasonable and not inflationary raises for the salaries of current faculty, so they were held to no more than fifteen percent of the 1942 salary.

By the spring of 1945, the school was crowded and needed another building to house a library, an adequate lunchroom, and a science laboratory. The board recognized that it could not install another temporary building and organized a Real Estate Committee to oversee plans for a stone building similar to Garrett. A Building Fund Campaign was begun in earnest in January of 1946, but ground could not be broken until the War Production Board lifted restrictions imposed to protect the supply and price of construction materials.[17] Unfortunately, the inflation that struck the nation had very real consequences for building plans at Bryn Mawr. Carmen Santos Randolph, Class of 1913 and longtime staff member, identified the situation well, noting, "What shall we do about the hockey fields? Last year the grass seed cost eighteen dollars. This year the same amount of seed will cost fifty."[18] Katharine Van Bibber found herself in the difficult situation of trying to hire new faculty at a time when young people had turned away from the teaching profession because there were other, better-paying opportunities; older teachers were either paid handsomely not to leave where they taught or needed pension contributions that Bryn Mawr could not afford. Baltimore was no longer a less expensive place to live than other eastern cities. The only recourse was to raise tuition, first in 1947 and again in 1948, to meet the rising costs of hiring good teachers. Finally, the school was able to offer competitive wages, and soon after both Roland Park Country and Garrison Forest Schools raised tuition and wages as well.

Over the years, Bryn Mawr had reorganized existing space, raised money, and deliberated the need for either a classroom building or for a gymnasium with a stage for performances. In 1948, plans to extend the east wall of Garrett were rejected when it was found that all the wiring for the building would have to be moved,

Handicrafts room for the Primary, 1940s

nearly doubling the original $10,000 estimate. Finally, in June of 1948, a one-story, stucco-covered building with an auditorium, stage, one or two classrooms, bathrooms, and a portico on the north side to create a covered walkway, was approved at a cost of $55,000. This building, dedicated on November 15, 1949, as the Elizabeth Smith Thomas Auditorium to honor Thomas' thirty-nine years of service to the school, was affectionately referred to as the ETA for many years of assemblies, plays, dinners, and dances. The ETA was the hub of school life for two generations of Bryn Mawr students; some of the structure is recognizable today as part of the cafeteria complex. The 406 students on campus in 1950–1951 were fortunate to also have a dedicated art studio added to the art and music complex, which was renovated in the summer of 2009 and now serves as classrooms for the fifth grade.

The spring of 1951 saw the demise of two well-established and popular girls' schools near Bryn Mawr as the result of financial instability. Girls' Latin, which had begun as a preparatory division of Goucher College in 1890, was a boarding and day school of national renown and competed early on with Bryn Mawr for studious Baltimore girls. Greenwood had been started in 1923 by Mary Elcock, director of athletics at Bryn Mawr for many years. After beginning at the William Buckler estate of Evergreen on North Avenue, the school bought a large property in Ruxton in 1926 and was known for its artistic and athletic activities, becoming famous for horsemanship and regular hunts featuring its own kennel of hounds.[19] Like Bryn Mawr, neither Girls' Latin nor Greenwood had an endowment; each was dependent on tuition, the generosity of donors, and frequently refinanced loans based on the few assets they owned to pay operating costs each year. As these reputable schools closed, Bryn Mawr was launching its first "Sustaining Fund" with the intention of raising several thousand dollars each year to add to the income from tuition to "pay better salaries, to give scholarships, and to put something aside for capital-improvements."[20] This "living endowment" model was in use by many colleges and universities to replace money for the annual budget that an invested endowment, which they could not quickly raise, would have provided from interest.

Boys had been severely restricted from entering the school grounds for anything other than graduation ceremonies since the school's founding. In early December of 1900, a crowd of boys had shown up on the rumor that they would be permitted to see a play, but were turned away. One clever fellow disguised himself in women's clothing and sneaked into the performance, only to be turned in by an audience member and locked up in an office to await Edith Hamilton. Newspapers from Baltimore to Burlington, Iowa, carried the story the next day of the boy's release by a kindhearted teacher after an anxious hour.[21] In *The Baltimore Sun* in 1948, Joseph Matthai recounted the frustration that he and his fellow students at Martson's University School for Boys had felt when barred fron Bryn Mawr events just across the street. One older boy disguised himself and managed to attend an early gymnasium exhibition. Another time, the boys closed the doors with ropes in protest, but the ropes were quickly cut and the boys still banned fron the event inside.[22] Boys were gradually admitted to outdoor athletic events, although space limitations kept them out of the gym for many years. Finally, in the winter of 1951, seven Gilman boys tromped the Bryn Mawr stage in a joint venture with eight girls of the Dramatic Club in "The Old Lady Shows Her Medals" and "Hands Across the Sea."[23]

The baby bust of the war years was now turning into a baby boom of the post-war era. By 1953–1954, there were forty-six girls in the fourth grade (Class of 1961) squeezed into three rooms in Gordon and headed for facilities the next year that could fit thirty-four at the most.[24] It was time to construct a new building and to redesign the existing space to accommodate the younger, larger classes coming up in the school. Work began in July, and the new spaces were ready by February of 1954. The Hamilton Building, originally named for the sisters who had served and led the school for many years, matched Garrett in style and construction and included its own bathrooms, a small kitchen, and the new senior room on the lower level, and two classrooms above that could hold the large Class of 1961 as Main I. One of the benefits of increased space was having a dedicated library for the first time since leaving Cathedral Street, rather than making do with shelves in departmental libraries and the small rooms at the back of the Study Hall. Once the seniors could

The Bryn Mawr School
DRESS REQUIREMENTS

	Each
4 Uniform Blue Jumpers with Emblem ....$ 7.95
6 Uniform White Shirts 3.25

For Athletics

2 Uniform Brown Gym Tunics and Bloomers 8.95
White Shirts
(Same as worn with Blue Jumper — one to be left in Locker for Gym. The Gym Department requires changing for health protection).
White socks only
(One extra pair to be kept in Locker).

ADDITIONAL NECESSITIES

1 Brown Shaker Slipover Sweater with Emblem 12.50
1 Navy Blue Cardigan Sweater for watching games 8.95
or
1 Navy Blue Heavy Shaker Slipover Sweater 12.50
6 Pairs White Socks .... .55
1 Pair Brown Oxfords or Saddle Shoes 9.95
1 Navy School Blazer (optional) 19.95
1 Brown School Blazer (optional) 19.95

THESE UNIFORMS ARE MADE IN STOCK SIZES ONLY

Uniform order form, 1950s

move into their new room, their former space was added to the library, which was redesigned to house the 5,000 volumes that had accumulated over the years, so that the girls no longer had to ask for help to reach the high shelves or sit on the floor to see the lower books.

The Supreme Court decision in Brown v. the Board of Education of Topeka, Kansas, on May 17, 1954, brought a new conversation to all schools in America. By law, schools receiving federal funding could no longer be segregated by race; the dual school systems, most predominant in the South existing under "separate but equal" conditions, would no longer be tolerated. Baltimore, although in close proximity to the North, was still essentially a city with southern roots and a large African American population residing primarily in distinct city neighborhoods. As much of the more affluent white population had moved to the northern edge of the city and the suburbs in the 1930s, the city center by the 1950s was becoming predominantly African American, and the two communities were isolated from each other. For some, this isolation was preferable, while others hoped for more interaction and an improvement in relations and opportunities. Bryn Mawr, along with other schools not receiving federal funding and thus not required to follow the Supreme Court ruling, would now need to make a policy decision on integration that would be both controversial and highly emotional for some members of its community. In January 1955, the board of managers began discussions about whether Bryn Mawr would integrate. It would take several years of conversation, deliberation, and consultation with the various constituencies of the school to come to a conclusion. The board resolved in November of 1956 that it would provide the school community eighteen months' notice before any change in the admissions policy regarding integration would go into effect. There were families who threatened to withdraw their children if the school integrated and others who lobbied the school to integrate quickly. In the spring of 1957, two respected teachers, Ruth Fiesel and Ann Merriam, resigned in frustration that the school was not moving faster toward integration.

As seniors, the Class of 1955 recognized how greatly the school needed a new, larger gymnasium, and after sharing their plan with Katharine Van Bibber, decided to launch a fund-raising effort by donating the balance of their treasury, $259.46, to initiate the Gym Fund. According to the headmistress, the showers had to be used as lockers, as there weren't enough lockers for everyone; the seating was so limited that only the upper school could watch games, leaving the younger girls out; students couldn't be scheduled for adequate time in the gym for physical education; and Bryn Mawr's competitors, most of which had large gyms on their campuses, could only bring a limited number of spectators.[25] After years of raising funds and changing plans, the Class of 1958 could finally watch the new gymnasium and cafeteria complex under construction through Hamilton's Senior Room windows.

Advances in technology, a greater awareness of America's role on the global stage, and a growing post-war economy contributed to new expectations of a high-school education. Before the "revolution in 1942," as Katharine Van Bibber referred to the change in the College Entrance Examination,[26] one significant way that independent schools distinguished themselves was through preparing students for the subject-oriented college entrance exams. The new SAT, however, required no specialized preparation. Independent schools found that they needed more than ever before to explain their value, as well as to expand their curricula. Released from the rigid structure of preparation for specific exams, and held to "no authority except to its own conscience and its own clientele" independent schools were free to choose any combination of ideas they wished for their students.[27] As they had found increased flexibility in the curriculum during and just after the war, independent schools faced new challenges found during the Cold War era. Bryn Mawr had always been focused on, "not merely with getting [the] girls into college, but with providing them with the means to grow, both in college and later, into creative and thoughtful citizens in a free American community."[28] The emphasis was on thinking and reasoning, and with greater freedom of choice in the curriculum there was more opportunity to encourage students to pursue additional courses in subjects that most interested them. An extra language, either Greek or German, could be taken; more music or art or a different placement in French, Latin, or mathematics were available to suit the needs of individual students. In 1956–1957, the one hundred and fifty-five girls in grades nine through twelve were following sixty-eight

Theodora Smith, teacher 1931–1961, director of the Primary School 1961–1966, with 4th-grade students in 1960. A niece of poet T.S. Eliot, she gave each of her students a copy of his book Old Possum's Book of Practical Cats, upon his death in 1965.

unique programs of study. French or German was taught every day for twenty minutes to students from kindergarten through sixth grade. By the time they reached the Main School, they would have had seven years of foreign language study as well as the required year of Latin in eighth grade.

Bryn Mawr had never sought accreditation from any agency, and the school had resisted pressure from families to do so over the years. In 1959, with more requests from parents to consider accreditation, Katharine Van Bibber addressed the issue in parent meetings, alumnae gatherings, and on the front page of the April Quill. Although both Gilman and Roland Park Country Schools had been accredited by the Middle States Association of Colleges and Secondary Schools, the headmistress and the board did not see a need for Bryn Mawr to join them, and neither did Garrison Forest nor St. Timothy's Schools. According to Katharine Van Bibber, accreditation in the region had begun in 1890 as part of an effort to raise the standards of the public schools, particularly those in rural areas. These schools, usually staffed by untrained instructors, were often only in session for the few winter months so that the children could work in the fields. To encourage schools to seek accreditation, certain member colleges agreed to admit the graduates of accredited schools without requiring entrance examinations. Since all Bryn Mawr School girls had to take the Bryn Mawr College entrance exams, and later the College Entrance Examination Board tests to graduate from the school, there was no benefit of accreditation for the students for college entrance, as there might be at other schools. Further, Bryn Mawr was not alone in resisting accreditation, since the students at St. Timothy's, Garrison Forest, and the Chapin and Brearley Schools in New York also applied to women's colleges that required entrance exams. They all declined to go through the accreditation process, which would divert too much time and energy of the faculty from their essential task of teaching their students. Bryn Mawr belonged to several educational associations that sponsored conferences, seminars, and workshops that the headmistress and faculty members could attend. Bryn Mawr was a member of the Head Mistresses Association of the East, the National Association of Principals of Schools for Girls, the National Council of Independent Schools, as well as the Private School Association of Baltimore. Katharine Van Bibber saw no compelling benefit for Bryn Mawr to become accredited by the Middle States Association at that time.

Class of 1959

By 1958, fully one-third of the students at Bryn Mawr were the daughters of alumnae, and almost one-third of the teachers were themselves alumnae of the school.[29] There were families for whom three generations and a wide array of relatives had attended the school. The girls spent their days together in class and studying, on the athletic fields and courts, at work on plays and community service projects, and outside of school at dances and social functions. They lived in the surrounding neighborhoods, which were predominantly white and Christian, and they attended many of the same churches and clubs. But society around them was changing, and it was time for Bryn Mawr to alter its admissions policy to reflect those changes. On January 30, 1962, the school announced in a letter to parents that beginning in September 1963, "All fully qualified applicants will be considered for admission to The Bryn Mawr School regardless of color."[30]

In the course of twenty-three years of leading the school, "throughout two decades of profound change, including depression, world war, cold war, and population explosion, the firm hand of Katharine Van Bibber had shaped the development of Bryn Mawr."[31] When she arrived in 1939, there were two hundred students using Gordon and its nearby kindergarten, the Gate House, the first section of the Garrett Building, and two temporary structures housing the gymnasium and study hall. "In those days prayers were held in the study hall, the lunch room was in the basement of the Garrett Building, the one small science laboratory was in the Gate House, and the art department had its studio in one of the small rooms on the first floor of the Gordon House." Under her leadership, the debt from moving to the Melrose campus was paid and a long-range building plan brought the construction of art and music studios, the Elizabeth Thomas Auditorium, the Hamilton Building, the office wing addition to the Garrett Building, and the new cafeteria and gymnasium, most appropriately named after Miss Van Bibber upon her retirement in 1962. The student body had tripled from two hundred to six hundred students in less than forty years. Famous for never wearing a coat, no matter the weather, and never closing school for snow, no matter how deep, Katharine Van Bibber was admired most by students for caring about the individual girls and their role in the school and in the greater community.

Kindergarten, 1960

Class of 1978 in 1st grade, 1966-1967

Chapter Five

BUILDING FOR BRYN MAWR 1962–1973

Alumnae visit Diane Howell's class, 1965

Diane Howell with Rosie

iane Howell was sought by four other schools as headmistress when she agreed to come to Bryn Mawr in July of 1962, a year in which no fewer than twenty-five girls' schools were seeking a headmistress. While she had no prior connection to Bryn Mawr, she was a graduate of the Northfield School for Girls in Massachusetts, as well as Barnard College. She served as an officer in the WAVES during World War II, taught English and history at The Winsor School in Boston and was the assistant to the headmistress at the Milton Academy Girls' School.[1] Katharine Van Bibber wrote to the alumnae that Diane Howell was the perfect choice for Bryn Mawr and that she was grateful to her for agreeing that the board's decision on integration be announced under Miss Van Bibber's tenure, as she felt deeply that integration was the right thing to do at Bryn Mawr.[2]

Diane Howell was experienced in the complex art of creating class schedules, but as she noted in her first address to the alumnae, printed in *The Bryn Mawr School Bulletin* in 1962–1963, "we can construct an ideal schedule on paper but cannot put it into operation because there are not enough rooms to accommodate the number of classes we should like to schedule for a given hour." There was not only a lack of classroom and art studio space; the Primary School was crowded into Gordon, and there was insufficient room in the library and the Study Hall, as well as for lockers and meetings. After studying how the school functioned during her first year as headmistress, she could reorganize existing space in Gordon by moving lunch to the Main School cafeteria for the third and fourth grades, providing room for a director's office, a teachers' room, a new second-grade classroom, an activities room, and space for a reading room. By combining kindergarten classes for the four- and five-year-olds, the Nurse's Office could be relocated so that students from the Main School would not have to walk through the Primary to see the nurse. Some shifting in the art studio gave Main II (sixth grade) a second day of art each week and allowed students in Main VI through VIII (tenth through twelfth grades), who were not able to take art classes because of the limited space, to work in the studio during their study periods if they wished. Moving lockers from the old gymnasium into the new one created the necessary space for a new elective history of art course for juniors and seniors.

Postwar development of education theory brought about a national reform movement in the 1950s and 1960s, the ideals of which were already in place at Bryn Mawr. Experts such as Paul Woodring, education editor of *The Saturday Review of Literature* and member of the Foundation for the Advancement of Education, proposed traditional Bryn Mawr practices such as early introduction to foreign languages, small class sizes, individualized instructional paths based on abilities and interests, team teaching, and greater academic challenge for college preparation.[3] The Ford Foundation invested some seventy million dollars from the 1930s through the 1960s to effect change in the education of teachers and the development of curricula which were now being implemented on campuses throughout the country. While Bryn Mawr had long been an innovator in progressive education, the school was always looking at new ideas and methods to see what it might choose to incorporate into the program. Changes in teaching methodology sent several Bryn Mawr teachers to summer school in 1963 to prepare for the "new" math, biology, and physics curricula, while new courses for seniors were developed to include Western political ideas and French civilization. The assembly program for the year was planned around the culture and history of the city of Baltimore and would eventually be incorporated in classroom instruction as well.

Within her first few months at Bryn Mawr, Diane Howell expressed her interest in not merely preparing the student for college and afterward, but also preparing her to contribute to the world around her, "giving freely, constructively, and wholeheartedly of herself."[4] Articles in *The Alumnae Bulletin* in the early 1960s reflect the mood of the nation, as alumnae reported on their service in the Peace Corps abroad and tutoring inner-city African American children through the Northern Student Movement.

Independent schools, as well as colleges and universities, were growing quickly in a booming postwar economy, and fund-raising took on a much larger, far-reaching goal for these nonprofit institutions. During the early 1960s, requests for financial support through the Annual Fund became more direct and more successful. At Commencement in 1965, the school could announce that more than $50,000 had been raised in only three months, entitling the school to an anonymous challenge gift of $100,000, more than tripling the amount raised in any previous Annual Fund campaign. In conjunction with this grant, a "Chair for Distinguished Teaching in English" was established and presented to Anita Marburg Lerner.

While the school had announced that it would accept applications from candidates without regard to race for the 1963-1964 school year, it was not until April of 1965 that Miss Howell could report that two African-American families interested in applying had visited the school. The biggest hurdle Bryn Mawr and other independent schools faced was finding candidates who were prepared academically for the college-preparatory program, as well as the cultural challenge of being the first to integrate the school. Marise Ross, a former local television reporter, had worked for several years with the Urban League in a program called "Tomorrow's Scientists and Technicians," or "TST," which took groups of talented students from predominantly African American junior and senior high schools to cultural and educational events that they would not otherwise have the opportunity to attend. Mrs. Ross went far beyond visits to the Lyric; she took her group, gifted and motivated students from Booker T. Washington Junior High School, PS 130, to meet politicians in Baltimore City Hall, the State House in Annapolis, and the United States Senate, where they witnessed Congress in the midst of the civil rights debate. They had behind-the-scenes meetings with actors and producers at Center Stage and Painters Mill Theatre, attended lectures at museums and colleges, and visited the United Nations and the World's Fair. In the spring of 1964, Mrs. Ross brought three of her gifted eighth graders to the attention of Friends, Park, and Notre Dame Preparatory Schools, where they entered in the fall with the help of a variety of scholarships.[5]

By 1965, Marise Ross organized a new group that she named "Training Now for Tomorrow" or "TNT." Operating on an extremely limited budget from donations, as well as some funding from the federal Upward Bound program, she was determined to introduce her young students to the independent schools and help them continue through college. She arranged for testing and interviews, bought the students clothes and books, and drove them everywhere in her car, which she filled with good books for them to borrow. The national press learned of her aim "to provide [students] with a cultural background, to open shut doors, to show them the wonders of exploring and reaching for their share," and she and her work were soon profiled in *Life Magazine* (October 8, 1965), the *Washington Post* (June 25, 1966), *Good Housekeeping* (October 1967), and on the "Today" show (January

Members of the Class of 1969 in 1967: Top: Susan Riley, Louise Woods, Bleigh Russum. Middle: Andrea Drozda, Sally Supplee, Mary Todd, Peggy Speas. Seated: Nancy Richardson, Lynn Tolley, Kathy Nixdorff, Cindy Clarke, Victoria Valsecchi

Lower School girls at play, late 1960s to early 1970s

Louise Brooks, Class of 1968, Leighton King, Class of 1969, and Dena Bright, Class of 1972

Erselle Datcher, Class of 1968

Primary carpool at the Gordon Building

1967.) By the time Diane Howell became a vice-president of the "TNT" Board in November 1967, Mrs. Ross was raising more than $35,000 annually on her own for her projects, but needed more funding to continue her work.

It was through Marise Ross that Bryn Mawr's first African American student, Erselle Datcher, Class of 1968, came to the school in the fall of 1965. Through the 1960s and early 1970s, several, but not all of Bryn Mawr's African American students were funded to some degree either through scholarships from the school or from funds arranged by TNT and other organizations. Erselle, who was elected president of the Athletic Association by her classmates, went on to Lake Forest College, where she earned a degree in psychology with special honors for her senior thesis on "Racial Preference and Awareness," and after graduation worked for the Urban League in Baltimore. She also served the school as a trustee for several years and spoke often with students about issues of race.[6]

The term "independent" was more commonly used by 1965 to describe what had previously been referred to as "private" schools. As Diane Howell explained in the *The Bryn Mawr School Bulletin* in the winter of 1965, usage had "changed not so much to avoid negative implications of the word 'private' as to suggest the positive qualities of the independent schools, schools born of freedom in a free society, schools committed to the preservation of freedom in that society." She described the misconception that independent schools were for wealthy or prominent families, who wanted to place their children with the "right" people, which was impossible in the increasingly mobile society of the 1960s. "A good independent school is independent in its choice of students; today it is looking for children of disparate social and economic backgrounds who have the necessary intellectual ability and curiosity, and the extremely important additional capacity for contributing something positive to the school." The increasing cost of running such an institution meant that every school, independent of any government funds, had to find ways to raise resources on its own through the dedication of alumnae, parents, and friends who believed in the mission, purpose, and program of the school. Diane Howell challenged the school community to consider the intrinsic value of a Bryn Mawr education beyond preparing girls for college. The world around them had changed rather drastically in the last several years because of the Cold War, the nuclear age, the Korean War and further conflict in Southeast Asia. Advancements in technology and telecommunication, men walking on the moon, racial conflict, and the assassination of a popular president were unsettling to many Americans. There was growing concern that the values and ethical fiber of youth prepare them to be leaders in a very uncertain future. Diane Howell believed that Bryn Mawr should teach its students the values of "generosity, tolerance, thoughtfulness, kindness, fair-play, self-sacrifice, of giving, of

Clare Hardy's science class, 1960

commitment to the good of mankind. These are the values which an independent school is free to believe in. They are not extra-mural or extra-curricular; they are an essential part of the curriculum of The Bryn Mawr School." In coming to Bryn Mawr, students had chosen to be members of a community that they also needed to serve, nurture, and respect, as part of learning to do the same for the larger world in which they lived.[7]

The baby boom continued, with record highs of public student enrollment noted again in 1964, and more students were coming to Bryn Mawr and to other nonpublic schools, both religious and independent, across the country. Dr. Benjamin Fine, the Pulitzer Prize-winning education editor of *The New York Times*, noted in 1965 that nationwide "an estimated 7,000,000 students attend these [nonpublic schools], or about 13% of the total school population." Predictions foresaw 15 to 20% nonpublic school enrollment nationally within a decade, with the "segregation issue" one of the prime factors for the increased enrollment.[8] In Baltimore, many families whose children might be forced to change schools and face busing to another part of the city sought out nonpublic schools for the first time, while others moved out of the city to predominantly white county schools, in a second

President of the Alumnae Association, Dorothy Wolff Phipps, Class of 1950; President of the Parents Association, Dorothea Stieff; and President of the Board of Trustees, Edith Hooper, at the Howell Center groundbreaking ceremony, February 23, 1968

wave of "white flight" that left the city with an increasingly smaller tax base to fund its school programs. "The loss of higher income families to the county," noted Dr. George B. Brain, retiring superintendent of schools, "is our major problem at the moment."[9] At the same time, the state superintendent of schools was warning state universities and colleges of an "acute need for teachers" in Maryland, as colleges and universities were turning out only one-third of the new teachers that the public schools would need. Maryland was "lagging behind many states in its quantitative emphasis on the production of teachers."[10] President Lyndon Johnson's "War on Poverty" would attempt to make education the "number one business of the American people" through Head Start and Title 1-funded programs aimed at improving the medical and educational situations of the youngest of the poor, primarily in inner cities such as Baltimore.[11] Government and non-government organizations established programs to assist inner-city Baltimore students with whom Bryn Mawr students, faculty, and alumnae would be involved for the next several decades.

The $8,000 raised at Bazaar in the spring of 1965 funded the construction of the Glass Room in time for the opening of school in September. Intended as a faculty dining room, it also provided space for board meetings and class teas, and it could be screened off as extra classroom space when needed. But an unprecedented gift of $500,000 in April of 1966, with pledges of another $100,000 from the members of the board and other friends of the school, meant that plans could be drawn up for a new "library-study-art center."[12] The new library was planned to hold thirty thousand books, and would be supplemented by a listening library of records and tapes, a microfilm reader for periodicals, slides for studying artwork, a photocopier, and films that could be viewed in the conference room. Comfortable chairs for informal reading as well as a room for typing papers were also included. Classrooms and an art studio were planned for the second floor. It was hoped that the space would "be a ringing memorial to the ideals and practices cherished by Edith Hamilton . . . for pursuing hard work and the concomitant joys of it which result in freeing individuals to live life rather than to spend it."[13]

Plans were being considered for a new Primary School building in the near future, but adequate facilities to teach science quickly took precedence. In 1966, a laboratory course in chemistry had to be added to the Upper School curriculum as it had become a college entrance requirement for students who desired a scientific or medical career. Fortunately, the Capital Fund Drive had been so successful that a building could finally be constructed with classroom and laboratory space for biology, chemistry, and physics. Classrooms were needed for the Mathematics Department, and offices for both the Math and Science Departments were included in the design, overseen by a science laboratory planning consultant from Boston. Clare Coriell Hardy, longtime science teacher and member of the Class of 1922, was delighted and honored when the building was named for her.

Biology, 1967

Bryn Mawr had been an active member of the Private Schools Association and the Teachers Association of the Independent Schools of the Baltimore Area. In 1967, these two groups merged to become the Association of Independent Maryland Schools, or AIMS, with Bryn Mawr as a founding member. The new organization provided statewide representation for all of its various members and sought to advance and strengthen independent schools while recognizing their individuality.[14]

Fund raising necessary for the new facilities was the impetus behind the first alumnae gatherings in New York, Boston, and Philadelphia, featuring Millicent Carey McIntosh and a viewing of the 1958 television interview of Edith Hamilton. The distinguished author John Mason Brown, longtime friend of Edith Hamilton and noted drama critic of *The Saturday Evening Review*, addressed the New York gathering where the announcement of the Edith Hamilton Memorial Fund for the new library was made. Memorial funds for other members of the school community were also established that year. Donors provided funds and photographic equipment to create a darkroom in the basement of the Gordon Building and to buy books for the new library. The first bequest program began in 1968, when several members of the board chose to include Bryn Mawr in their wills. The Class of 1969, seeking to contribute to the library in its own way, challenged the Gilman seniors to a fundraising basketball game and won, 38 to 34. The *News American* jokingly noted that it "has reportedly shaken the very underpinnings of Baltimore's scholastic-athletic superstructure." The May *Quill*, however, admitted that there may have been some favoritism shown by the referee, Miss Norma Simmons, and expressed hope that wrestling wouldn't be the next coeducational endeavor.[15]

On April 24, 1968, the senior class volunteered to teach at Bryn Mawr for the day, so that the faculty could observe other schools in the city as part of several programs of outreach to community projects.[16] To experience a bit of the adult world they were preparing to enter, the seniors in the Class of 1969 spent ten days at the end of May in either individual pursuits or in small groups in a variety of senior projects. Some worked in advertising, prepared surveys, taught in a school, or staffed offices of public officials in Washington, D.C., and at Baltimore City Hall. Five of the girls worked on an Appalachian demonstration farm in Walker, Kentucky, planting 21,000 hot peppers, picking strawberries and rhubarb, and doing other agricultural chores.[17]

Nancy Coale Baker, Class of 1967, center, and classmates

Unrest and conflict at colleges and universities in America and abroad at the end of the 1960s resulted from student frustration with the established order, both on and off campus. Student groups arranged protests, took over administration buildings, and refused to attend classes, demanding greater voice and more choice in their education, and marking their displeasure in political policy. A report by Harvard overseers in September of 1969 noted that the draft had made the growing unrest felt by students over the Vietnam conflict more concrete, and that "concern with racial discrimination and newly intensified awareness of other kinds of social injustice added to the feeling of many students that society as now constituted required basic change."[18] Persistence and determination by students led to their greater involvement in decision-making on campuses and closer communication with institutional administrators. Revamped curriculum included greater emphasis on political inequity and discrimination, and the development in particular of African American studies, and increased enrollment of minorities in institutions nationwide.

Diane Howell told the board in a report in 1971 that "what is happening in the universities is filtering down to our young in schools–even to the very young. We must find ways to respond to their needs." Writers noted in *The Quill* that many institutions lacked the kind of student government and forums available to students at Bryn Mawr, where they could voice their opinions freely but respectfully in the classrooms and invite speakers from a variety of viewpoints. On October 15, 1969, Bryn Mawr participated in the national moratorium for Vietnam by holding school, but bringing in speakers to talk about the war and lead a series of conversations about it. Students and faculty could then join the groups convening downtown.[19] Campus unrest disappeared from the news in autumn of 1971, perhaps affected by the lowering of the voting age to 18 in July, thus providing college students and many high school seniors with a voice in the process for the upcoming election year.

Both societal and financial pressures caused many single-sex colleges and universities across the country to announce in 1968–1969 that they would soon change to some form of coeducation.[20] Brown and Pembroke, Columbia and Barnard, and Harvard and Radcliffe had already become coordinate colleges, allowing two separate institutions to continue to operate, while enjoying the benefits of some shared courses, faculty, and resources. Yale and Vassar spent several months considering either a merger or coordination before they each chose coeducation instead, and Wellesley and the Massachusetts Institute of Technology experimented with sharing courses. Amherst, Princeton, and Johns Hopkins were among many other colleges which deliberated their options for quite a while before permitting a limited number of women to enroll. In July of 1969, *The Sun* reported that "more than 53 colleges and universities are becoming coeducational or have such plans under consideration."[21]

Independent schools were facing the same decreasing enrollments coupled with rising operating costs that colleges were trying to address. According to the National Association of Independent Schools, twenty-four private schools had closed in just a few short years before 1972, and "almost half the schools responding to a 1971 NAIS questionnaire said that they were operating at a deficit." In the six years from 1965 to 1971, 410 Catholic elementary and secondary schools closed on average per year as well, dropping from 13,292 to 10,829.[22] Further proof of the declining interest in independent schools was a near twenty-five-percent drop

Georgia D. Smith, Class of 1972, emerging from Study Hall

in the number of students taking the Secondary School Aptitude Test between 1969 and 1972.[23] To attract more students, independent schools across the country responded to societal changes and relaxed their rules on mandatory chapel and sports, dropped uniform and strict dress codes, and added more electives and independent study to their curricula. Admissions directors updated their brochures and applications and began to actively recruit students from feeder schools; many boarding schools took in day students for the first time. Similar to many of their college counterparts, some single-sex independent schools became coeducational, both to enlarge the pool of

Reading Room, Howell Library, 1970s

qualified applicants and to avoid losing good applicants who preferred a coeducational school. In 1968, the Choate and Rosemary Hall Schools announced that the latter would sell its Greenwich, Connecticut campus and move to the boys' school in Wallingford to open in the fall of 1971 as a merged school. Rosemary Hall Headmistress Alice E. McBee noted in *The New York Times* article covering the change that "independent education is facing a crisis, and if it is to remain strong, this, we believe is the way." The article goes on to point out that not only do shared resources lower costs, but that "girls' schools generally find it hard to compete in fund drives with the schools that get husbands' contributions," an issue that development officers of girls' schools have grappled with for decades.[24] "Even when the woman outlives the man, she usually ends up bequeathing her estate to his school," commented an administrator at the Emma Willard School in a front page *Wall Street Journal* article about the changes private schools made in "fighting to stay alive."[25] The already declining enrollment at girls' boarding and day schools was exacerbated as formerly all-male schools such as Andover, Exeter, St. Paul's (New Hampshire), Groton, and Hotchkiss became new options for girls around the country. The Baldwin School in Bryn Mawr, Pennsylvania, chose in 1972 to stop taking boarding students, graduating the last boarders in 1974. Many students chose to apply to the boarding schools of their fathers and brothers, the traditional feeders for the formerly all-male Ivy League. Locally, McDonogh, where operating deficits had tripled in one year from $50,000 in 1969–1970 to $150,000—and were projected to be $250,000 the following year—dropped its long-standing military tradition in 1971. It faced the dilemma of all schools of "how much higher we can raise tuition without pricing ourselves out of the market."[26] McDonogh opened enrollment to girls in 1975. Bryn Mawr held fast to its role in providing a singular education for girls, as did other strong girls' schools around the country that were determined to find the finances to continue on their own.

The Maryland State Board of Education was taking greater interest in independent schools and in the qualifications of their faculties, as part of the ongoing educational reform movement. Independent schools were not required to hire certified teachers, and so they were free to choose subject experts for their classrooms, bringing a greater variety of academic and professional backgrounds and expertise. While many Bryn Mawr teachers were certified, Diane Howell related that she would be the least-qualified teacher at Bryn Mawr by the state's standards and would need to take eighteen credits of coursework to qualify "as a teacher, much less as a principal." She also noted that over the years, she had replaced the largely part-time teachers she found when she arrived with full-time faculty with classroom experience.[27] Bryn Mawr would become certified by the state in March of 1969, and Diane Howell believed that the time had come to consider accreditation by the Middle States Association, but she felt that the school should wait until the association had completed revising its accreditation manual.

Lower School in the Gordon Building, circa 1970

The need for a new Lower School building was becoming acute by 1969. The Gordon Building could no longer hold the number of students and their activities appropriately, and worse, the fire marshal objected to students on the upper floors of the old former residence. The Lower School faculty had researched and begun to develop programs for a proposed open space building and team teaching. Students enjoyed moving more independently through their material under the guidance of their teachers, while the teachers realized that with the new method, fourth-grade math students covered fifty percent more material than had been covered in the previous unit. In anticipation of new space, the board announced that the Kindergarten Class, which had been eliminated in 1967 because of space restrictions and decreasing enrollment, would be reinstated in the fall of 1971. Bryn Mawr had been extremely successful with the "Master Plan for Capital Improvement," which had been developed in 1967, raising $1,800,000 in four years, making the school one of the leaders in the area in raising capital funds. Although Bryn Mawr surpassed its goal of $250,000 to obtain a challenge gift of $500,000 from an anonymous foundation to build the new Lower School, another $110,000 was still needed, but construction could finally begin.[28]

Lower School complex, 1972

In 1972, the three one-story open space buildings, designed by noted Swiss Bauhaus architect Marcel Breuer, were ready for the Lower School students. As Edith Ferry Hooper, the board member who had been instrumental in bringing Mr. Breuer to the project was quoted as saying in *The Baltimore Sun*, Bryn Mawr's goal was "not to build just another lower school, but a lower school that was utterly adjustable to the future. The feeling was that architecture is just as much education as books or music, that a building is an educational thing."[29]

After three decades serving as the home of the dwindling German Singing Societies, Mary Garrett's massive structure on Cathedral Street, built so lovingly for Bryn Mawr, was facing the wrecking ball. The paperwork to nominate the building as an official landmark was not processed in time. With little purpose left for the outdated, high-maintenance building, there was nothing to do but bear witness as it came down in December 1972.[30] Everything that could be carried out of it was sold or taken as souvenirs, but it was through the quick action of four alumnae, Mary Hardy, Class of 1916, Clare Hardy, 1922, Dorothy Levering Packard, 1914, and Elizabeth Packard, 1925, that The Bryn Mawr School mosaic, that had graced the entrance of the building since 1890, was salvaged and brought to the Melrose campus in January of 1973.[31] The mosaic was installed in front of the Owl Gate between the Hamilton and Garrett Buildings and serves as a lasting reminder of the many Bryn Mawr girls who have crossed over it through the years.

The mosaic arrives at the Melrose campus, 1973

In the fall of 1972, Goucher College senior Kate Edmunds, Bryn Mawr Class of 1969, observed 9th-and 12th-grade classes at the school and noted how much the emphasis had shifted from lectures to classroom discussions, and that the students assumed a more active role in their education than just a few years earlier. She wrote to alumnae in *Communiqué* that she found that students were more independent in choosing their activities, volunteer projects, and extracurricular roles, both on and off campus, leading to more self-reliance in preparation for college.[32]

Three generations of Bryn Mawr Careys: Georgia D. Smith, Class of 1972, Mary Louise Carey Smith, Class of 1950, Millicent Carey McIntosh, Class of 1916, and Deirdre Smith, Class of 1978

The Carey Seminar, established by the board of trustees in 1972, "Honored Margaret Thomas Carey and her daughter Millicent Carey McIntosh of the Class of 1916, whose combined service to the school had spanned most of the century."[33] Each of the women had been significantly responsible for the survival and continued success of the school during some of its most critical times. Millicent Carey McIntosh also was honored as Bryn Mawr's first trustee emerita. The seminar has brought many noted speakers to campus over the years since April of 1973, including the presidents of Johns Hopkins, Barnard, and Radcliffe, and experts in education theory, law, and finance.

Lower School girls at play, 1970s

Chapter Six

BUILDING COMMUNITY 1973–1980

Members of the Class of 1978: Donna Peregoff, Barbara Van Cutsem, and Carey Hoff, 1976

*I*n a letter to the board of trustees in September of 1972, Headmistress Diane Howell explained that she would step down from her position effective July 1, 1973. A *Baltimore Sun* article quoted her as writing, "I have concluded that the coming academic year should be my last. Much that I had hoped for 10 years ago will have been accomplished . . . and in retrospect, I should like to think of my tenure as a decade of 'building for Bryn Mawr.'"[1] President of the Board Dorothy Richardson noted that the new Library-Art-Study Center (which would soon be named the Diane Howell Library), the Clare Coriell Hardy Science Building, and the Lower School complex would "serve as lasting reminders of the broad vision of [Howell's] leadership." During her ten-year tenure, the Endowment Fund had increased tenfold and the Annual Giving Program had grown to make up much of the difference between tuition income and the cost of operating the school.[2] Diane Howell had also overseen the integration of the school, brought a greater sense of community service to the students, and begun the work of making the curriculum more liberal and flexible, including the planning of coordination with Gilman and open space teaching in the Lower School.[3]

The Search Committee chose Blair Danzoll Stambaugh, a classicist at Williams College, as the next headmistress for Bryn Mawr. A Wheaton College graduate with graduate studies at Smith, she had taught Latin and Greek at the Abbot Academy, and Latin, English, and history at the Pine Cobble School in Williamstown, Massachusetts. She also was greatly involved in the Young Women's Christian Association, serving as the vice-chairman of the National Student YWCA, and as a member of the National Board.[4] In May of 1973, Bryn Mawr purchased 5613 Boxhill Lane for $70,000 as a residence for the school's headmistresses, to provide a suitable home for entertaining and holding small meetings.

Blair D. Stambaugh

There were several new plans in place for the fall of 1973. Bryn Mawr and Gilman formalized curriculum coordination by changing to a shared six-day class cycle and building twelve minutes into the schedule between classes for walking between campuses. Initially, Bryn Mawr seniors went to Gilman for advanced Spanish, math, and some English electives, while Gilman students took German and electives in French, history, and English at Bryn Mawr. All the Spanish courses were then taught at Gilman, and all the German courses were at Bryn Mawr. Changing from a semester to a trimester system the following year also created opportunities for many juniors and seniors to take classes on the other campus.

Another significant change in 1973 came with the realignment of the academic divisions at Bryn Mawr. The new buildings allowed Main I, now known as the fifth grade, to move out of the Main School and into the new Lower School Elementary Center, together with grades two, three, and four. Kindergarten and first grade moved into the new Primary Center. There was now an opportunity to establish formally a new Middle School composed of grades six, seven, and eight (previously named Mains II, III, and IV). This would allow a faculty dedicated to the middle grades to develop curriculum and activities better suited to young teens, under the leadership of Director of the Middle School Janet Barnitz. As the younger members of the Main School, these students had been left out of much of the leadership and extracurricular activity that was dominated by the older girls. These middle schoolers would now have their own drama, art, and sports organizations. They could develop their own literary publications and community service projects that would be better adapted to their skills and interest levels and, most importantly, they could build their own sense of identity on The Bryn Mawr School campus. Within four years, the Middle School had successfully instituted an integrated arts program within the curriculum, which also included 6th-grade physics, 7th-grade biology, and 8th-grade earth science. French and German were offered, with Latin required in the 8th grade and a Greek course offered for the first time in 7th grade in 1978–1979. Middle School now had its own chorus and handbell group, a literary magazine called the *Magpie*, and presented its own Christmas pageant. Coordination among Middle School music, art, and drama instruction brought every Middle School student on stage in March of 1978 in a very successful presentation of the musical *Oliver*.[5] Middle School faculty shared their outside interests with students during weekly activity periods. Cooking with Headmistress Blair Stambaugh was a popular activity.

Lower School math class, 1975

Between 1960 and 1973, the number of women's colleges had dropped from 300 to 146, and men's colleges from 261 to 101. Nationwide, the high school graduating class of 1973 was the largest ever in history, but for the first time in twenty-eight years, overall enrollment had declined, with elementary school enrollment declining for the fourth consecutive year.[6] In Baltimore, *The Sun* reported that the city was "losing about 5,000 elementary students annually," but noted that the resultant surplus of teachers provided public schools with an opportunity to improve education to "individualize instruction and to experiment with open learning... [and] concentrate at least the same number of dollars on fewer pupils."[7] Independent schools looked to the colleges' survival tactics of cutting costs by joining other institutions in consortia for purchasing health insurance and other benefits and supplies. The former head of McDonogh, Dr. Robert L. Lamborn, became the first director of the Council for American Private Education (CAPE), to serve as a "point of contact between the government and over 5,000,000 private school children," or ten percent of all elementary and secondary students in the country. CAPE also would provide annual statistics on nonpublic school student demographics, which at that point had only been produced every five years, as the government debated forced busing, continued desegregation plans, and tax ramifications for nonpublic schools.[8]

Rising inflation coupled with declining enrollment was creating a fiscal crisis for nonpublic colleges and schools. Overall, the cost of basic supplies continued to increase, but the 1974 oil embargo against the United States was driving utilities and heating fuel costs to unseen heights. In a plea to the state for more assistance, a group of private Maryland colleges noted that "while the consumer price index has increased 41 percent since 1971, utility costs at the association schools have jumped 135 percent."[9]

This led to the formal establishment of a Development Office at Bryn Mawr in 1976–1977, quartered in the Old Office Building (today's Garrett Annex), which allowed for focused fund-raising. Within three years, donors had given more than one million dollars, tripling the endowment from $320,000 to approximately one million in 1979.[10] The "Bryn Mawr Way" campaign raised funds from a variety of sources, including foundations that provided funds for scholarships and improved teacher compensation, which had fallen below the average statistics of the National Association of Independent Schools. Nationwide, independent schools had realized that they needed the financial support of institutions beyond the charitable abilities of community families and alumnae.[11] Thirteen area independent schools also joined together to form the Baltimore Independent School Scholarship Fund, to provide a means to request funding from local businesses that previously had not donated to the independent schools. This group would share donated funds to provide scholarship support for Baltimore City children to attend the member schools. In 1977, Bryn Mawr was chosen to receive annual scholarship assistance from the endowment fund of the Samuel Ready School, which had closed after 113 years.[12] Other donations endowed the Alumnae Science Chair and the Cynthia LeBoutillier Memorial Fund to provide support for a beginning Bryn Mawr teacher, preferably an alumna of the school.

At a special meeting on February 16, 1977, the board approved plans to open a coeducational pre-kindergarten program at Bryn Mawr in the fall, for children aged two to five. Rather than a day care center, the Bryn Mawr Little School was to be "an educational facility for children needing a full-day program," with an extended day program available for younger schoolchildren. The project had been in development since the fall of 1976, when an anonymous donor provided initial funding. As Little School Director Jean Hawley described it in 1978, the Little School, "a logical outgrowth of Bryn Mawr's traditional concern for educated women, was conceived as a means of enabling young women to pursue careers or high-level volunteerism by making available a facility in which their children could receive quality education and care."[13] Within a year of opening, plans were made to expand from the original twenty children to forty.

Throughout the early-to-mid-1970s, the city of Baltimore was still struggling to meet federal requirements for school integration with a city population that was predominantly African American. Even if the city could reassign all of the students throughout the public schools, the resultant 70 percent African American enrollment still would "be construed as racial isolation."[14] The courts had ruled that cities could not force nearby county school systems with predominantly white students to help them integrate. Attempts at forced busing that sent children across the city were altered by a ruling that children could not be bused beyond two schools from their homes, and attempts to maintain some open enrollment transfers within the city were denied. At the same time, schools were struggling to maintain their academic standards amid teacher strikes, overcrowded classrooms, and declining funds. Between 1973 and 1975, the drop in enrollment in the city's public schools was fifty percent greater than the decline in the numbers of school-age children in Baltimore. For the first time, a notable increase in African American families moving out of the city to the nearby counties was recorded, with anecdotal evidence that they were leaving a school system in chaos.[15] While enrollment was declining nationwide in public schools, Baltimore's drop of sixteen percent from 1972 to 1977 was much higher than the national average. AIMS noted a two percent increase in enrollment among its member schools, which was double the national average. Blair Stambaugh told *The Sun* in November of 1978 that "It's fair to say that more people are applying from Baltimore city public schools than in the past. The numbers are not huge but they are far more than ever before. There's reluctance on the part of some of these parents, who say they believe in public school but feel compelled to look elsewhere." The article went on to note that "minority enrollments [in nonpublic schools] alone have quadrupled nationally in the last ten years. Today . . . fully seven percent are from minority groups. That stacks up well against both the public system and much of higher education."[16]

Peter Warren teaching class, 1981

The Rosabelle Sinclair Athletic Fund was established to raise $50,000 in honor of Miss Sinclair and to name the Upper Field in recognition of her contributions to the development of the physical education program.[17] The same year also brought a $50,000 grant from the Ensign C. Markland Kelly Jr. Memorial Foundation in support of Bryn Mawr athletics. Ensign Kelly had been an athlete in three Baltimore independent schools in his youth, before losing his life in World War II. In the fall of 1977, Bryn Mawr dedicated the Lower Field in his memory.

Although enrollment at Bryn Mawr was up in 1977, all the predictions and statistics about falling birthrates and increasingly difficult financial times ahead for the nation required the school to take a good look at the direction in which it was heading. The board of trustees established the Long-Range Planning Committee in the spring of 1976 to consider whether the school was "making the most productive use of its financial, physical, and human resources" and whether the "founding principles and goals" could carry the school securely into its next century. The school's first philosophy statement, what is known today as a mission statement, came from the board's desire to describe the strong history and tradition of the school.

Lower School teacher, former trustee, and honorary alumna Kitty Washburne working with students, 1975

Bryn Mawr hosted one of a series of NAIS conferences entitled "Women in Leadership" sponsored by the Task Force on Women in Education in April of 1977.

Funding also was obtained for an expanded studies program in the Lower School, in which students spent their afternoons exploring topics in archaeology, math, and history. The Geraldine R. Dodge Foundation provided resources for a "City as Learning Laboratory" program in the Upper School in June of 1979. The Edward E. Ford Foundation awarded the school a three-year grant for Upper School faculty evaluation and development, which also supported a campus-wide self-evaluation study in 1979. After years of choosing not to be accredited by outside associations, Bryn Mawr recognized that it was now time to do so.

In September 1977, the Education Committee of the board had found that although accreditation was both expensive and time-consuming, other schools had found the self-examination to be beneficial to their institutions. Kitty Washburne, director of the Lower School, asked the Pennsylvania Association of Private Academic Schools (PAPAS) to evaluate the Lower School as the one institution outside the state that it would work with that year. The Middle School joined the evaluation, as did the Little School, although it had not been in existence long enough to receive a formal assessment. The report PAPAS gave the school was laudatory of the program, and the organization was thankful for the privilege of being part of the school's progress.[18] Bryn Mawr would receive its first accreditation by the Middle States Association of Colleges and Schools in 1979.

Roland Park Country School announced in 1977 that it had purchased the twenty-one-acre former Doehme estate on Roland Avenue and would move in the fall of 1979, after building its new campus. Fire had destroyed the school's most recently constructed building on its sixty-year-old campus at 817 West University Parkway during the Thanksgiving weekend in 1976, and the school had continued in the buildings that were left while seeking new quarters. The former school site is now the home of Roland Park Place, a residence for senior citizens where several Bryn Mawr alumnae and retired teachers live today.

Thekla M. FitzPatrick, Class of 1951 and teacher of French for nearly twenty years, was the first recipient of the Millicent Carey McIntosh Chair in the Humanitites in February of 1978. The honor is bestowed "upon a member of the faculty whose teaching abilities, distinction in her field, and concern for the special educational needs of girls reflect the tradition of Millicent McIntosh."[19]

On September 25, 1979, the board of trustees reluctantly accepted the resignation of Blair Stambaugh effective July 1, 1980. She wrote that she was "satisfied with her contributions to Bryn Mawr and her sincere feeling that this is a good time for new leadership to come to Bryn Mawr." Diane Howell had overseen the extensive planning and construction of the school's physical needs. In her seven-year tenure,

Trustee Betsy Strobel Wilgis, Class of 1958

Blair Stambaugh had focused on building a strong community base and developing a sound financial foundation. Betsy Strobel Wilgis, Class of 1958 and president of the board, noted that she was a "builder of people during her tenure rather than a builder of buildings." Mary K. McPherson, director of the Upper School, wrote that "it was Blair's outstretched hand that brought home again so many [alumnae] who had long been out of touch with the School." She also had brought more public attention to the school through the development of new programs and her participation in associations and organizations on a national level. Coordination with Gilman and the new Little School were both well established and quite successful, as were her efforts to improve faculty development and evaluation. In recognition of her work, the Blair D. Stambaugh Award was established "to honor a member of the faculty or staff who has contributed the most to the overall welfare and well-being of the School community."[20]

Gatehouse, 1970s

Top: Mira Kautzky, Jennie Ness, and
Dena Dudgeon, Class of 1988

Left: Members of the Class of 1991 in third
grade: Anike Edmonds, Erika Murray,
Alexandra Stuehler, Mimi Vishio, Jenny Keyser,
Margaret Coulbourn

1980

Outdoor coordinated class in front of the Study Hall, 1980s

Chapter Seven

NO ONE EVER REALLY LEAVES BRYN MAWR 1980–1994

Vanessa Harmatz, Paola Sansur, and Julie Rubin, Class of 1991

arbara Landis Chase, Upper School history teacher and director of admission at the Wheeler School in Rhode Island, accepted the board's offer to serve as the next headmistress of Bryn Mawr in 1980. She brought with her experience teaching in Lower, Middle, and Upper Schools, as well as a background in music and choral programs. Known as a creative problem solver, confident, bright, and committed to strong academics, Barbara Chase balanced the educational interests of the school with its practical needs.

Bryn Mawr was not immune from the challenges facing independent schools across the country in the early 1980s, beginning above all else with the need for fiscal strength and a balanced budget in a floundering economy. The recession of the late 1970s, driven in part by oil embargoes in 1974 and 1979, had increased heating and transportation costs and thus the price of consumer goods nationwide, bringing double-digit inflation by 1980. The cost of nearly everything the school purchased rose dramatically in a span of just a few years. Rapid advances in technology, which had not been included in any school's budget just three years earlier, now necessitated careful and judicious decision-making in the purchase or lease of equipment and software. And, while Bryn Mawr had successfully constructed several buildings in the past two decades, the physical plant needed considerable preventative maintenance to avoid greater and now more costly repairs. As the director of admission at a Connecticut boarding school would explain, "the siege of inflationary recession provided us a common challenge–survival. In private schools, as well as in public schools, programs have been slashed, plant use curtailed, teachers let go."[1] The wildly shifting economy drove families to default on their enrollments at boarding schools across the country as they opened in September of 1982. Several small New England schools had as many as thirty to forty students withdraw over the summer. As schools turned to their waiting lists, belatedly accepted students then reneged on the schools where they had agreed to enroll, creating a ripple effect which ultimately affected many day schools.[2]

Despite financial hardship, independent schools survived through their ability to respond quickly to the calls for a return to traditional values and a strong core curriculum, for which Bryn Mawr was already widely recognized. As public school systems struggled with dwindling budgets, declining SAT scores, newly imposed competency exams in most states, and continued threats of redistricting and busing, enrollment at independent schools nationwide rose despite increasing tuition

Barbara Landis Chase

costs. Enrollment of both minority students and children of two-income families was at an all-time high in independent schools and notably included more children of public school teachers.[3] At a time of concerted budget cutting, Bryn Mawr would continue to balance cost effectiveness with the mission of the school to provide an outstanding educational experience. Barbara Chase emphasized that Bryn Mawr had always been committed to doing what was best for the academic program rather than compromise its ideals and mission.

Barbara Chase also brought a keen sense of community building to Bryn Mawr, strengthening relationships between the school and its various constituencies, among the academic divisions on campus, and with the city of Baltimore and farther afield. Students, families, and alumnae were informed about activities at the school through a monthly newsletter begun in the fall of 1981. They read of frequent performances by the Cambrian Choir and the school's string players throughout the city, and middle school students volunteering in nursing homes through Magic Me. Juniors and seniors in the Gold Key Club began to conduct tours for prospective families to provide a student's point of view of the school. Students helped to maintain the school through a work program, contributing to Bryn Mawr's upkeep while reducing operating expenses by working at the switchboard, proctoring, or helping in the Little School and after-school programs. Students also served on several trustee committees to provide their perspective on current issues that affected them. In the winter of 1982, Barbara Chase began the first of her Brown Bag Lunches in her office in the Gordon Building to enable parents to join her for conversation about education and the school. In 1984, members of the board began to host the lunches in their offices downtown to accommodate working parents and alumnae. These gatherings proved so popular that they continued past her tenure into 1996.

The new Middle School advisory system instituted in 1980–1981, in which each teacher served as an advisor, was deemed an immediate success, as was the new house system. The entire Middle and Upper Schools were grouped into houses named after six significant women in the school's history: Janet Barnitz, Mary Elizabeth Garrett, Edith Hamilton, Claire Hardy, Rosabelle Sinclair, and M. Carey Thomas. The houses were created to improve school spirit and give students the opportunity to interact across classes and divisions. Each house had a senior who served as captain, a junior who was vice captain, and a middle school captain from the eighth grade, as well as faculty members. The twelve house captains were also

Nina Colhoun, Class of 1984, Rebekah Lord, Class of 1982, and Margaret Gatchell, Class of 1982, wearing Garrett House sweaters on an inter-house field day in 1981

leaders of the Student Government Association. The first inter-house field day brought the houses together in friendly competition, as well as for community building events such as planting bulbs throughout campus. Students could earn points for their house through the year by participating in a variety of events and campus activities.[4] The house system was somewhat similar to the intramural teams that the school created in 1907, after great discouragement from losing the basketball game to St. Timothy's. The school had been divided into two teams to increase the competition and level of skill in the only sport Bryn Mawr played against any outside team at the time. Members could earn or lose points for their team based on other school activities as well.[5]

Running a nonprofit independent school was a constant struggle to manage increasing costs while keeping tuition affordable. In the decade leading to the early 1980s, the financial aid program had grown from $30,000 to $100,000, and the number of current students who could receive full or partial tuition grants based on demonstrated financial need and availability of funds doubled from thirty to sixty. A competitive scholarship exam was established to provide funds to three new students, and a new parent loan program was added in 1983 to provide funding for Upper School students. The increase in funds available was one reason that enrollment in nonpublic schools was up fourteen percent nationally. Enrollment in member schools of the Association of Independent Maryland Schools was increasing two percent annually, at a time when public school enrollments were declining at a similar pace. The College Board reported that the income of the families of graduates of independent schools was dropping. Sarah Ann M. Donnelly, the director of AIMS, noted that independent schools worked "to educate the whole child, building a curriculum around not just academic subjects, but moral responsibility and extracurricular activities as well." Independent schools offered small class sizes, a traditional curriculum, a greater rate of diversity than found in public schools, and the opportunity for single-sex education.[6]

By 1982, the Bryn Mawr admissions policy included a non-discriminatory state
ment in regard to "race, color, national, and ethnic origin." Bryn Mawr, Friends,
Gilman, and Roland Park Country Schools joined together to form the Baltimore
Project for Black Students as an adjunct of the Black Student Fund of Washington,
D.C., with the project director based at Bryn Mawr. The project mission was to assist
African American families interested in independent schools by providing information and referral services, and counseling them through the admissions process and
beyond enrollment. They also sought to help schools attract and employ a more
diverse workforce.[7]

Technology became increasingly important in the early 1980s for both the educational and administrative concerns of the school. The complexity of managing
school finances, communications, personnel records, fund-raising, and alumnae
information grew with each year. By the spring of 1980, requests for accounting
and word processing, as well as trained administrative staff, were made from offices
throughout the campus. The first microcomputers to arrive at Bryn Mawr were gifts
from the parents; one in the Lower School as tribute to the retiring director, Kitty
Washburne, and one in the Upper School to replace the rented terminal that provided expensive access to a mainframe at Johns Hopkins University. In the spring of
1983, Bryn Mawr held Microfest, a computer fair cosponsored by Apple Computer,

*Andrea Leand, Class of 1981,
and Page Ward, Class of 1982,
in the Senior Room*

that brought children and adults to campus from all over Baltimore. A program funded by the Geraldine R. Dodge Foundation in 1982, which brought Goucher College math and technology students to Bryn Mawr daily to mentor the girls, grew into a joint Summertech program to work with middle school-aged girls in science and technology.[8] Eight major studies of American high schools were published in 1983, including one by Dr. Theodore R. Sizer, who advocated teaching students how to learn; "if you know how to learn, then you can set about getting any information you need, in any subject."[9] Also in 1982, sixth- and seventh-grade students who were particularly strong in math began working with an Upper School math teacher on concepts that were not part of the regular Middle School curriculum. In June 1984, Bryn Mawr was the only independent school among fifteen colleges and universities to be given an Exceptional Achievement Award from the Council for Advancement and Support of Education for its programs with Goucher.[10]

As part of an effort to include real world learning in the classroom, economics became a natural focus throughout the school in the spring of 1982, as the Carey Seminar brought four experts in economics and finance to campus. Financial consultant and Bryn Mawr parent Howard P. Colhoun, and the senior economist of the World Bank, Dr. Sherman Robinson, who developed an economics game for the entire school to play, brought global money issues to campus. Economics was taught as a course in the Upper School and was explored in the Lower School's Expanded Studies program. The Middle School spent two "zero days" investigating financial and other features of the can industry as part of its Baltimore City studies, visiting manufacturing and labeling plants, as well as recycling centers.

Lower School student Mary Jo Geyer, Class of 1989, working on an Apple II computer

In 1983, Goucher College contracted with Bryn Mawr to operate a branch of the Little School program on its Towson campus. Although it was highly successful, space constriction on the Goucher campus forced the closing of the Little School program at Goucher fifteen years later, in 1998. Many of the young students would enter the Little School on the Bryn Mawr campus.

The Lucy Eastwood Broadus Memorial Award was established in 1983 by the Broadus family to provide the opportunity for a dedicated member of the faculty or administration to travel in the summer. The first recipient was English teacher Elizabeth Diamond, who wrote about her travels in France in the school *Newsletter* of November 1984. Twenty-five years later, the award winners typically make a multimedia presentation for the entire faculty and staff, complete with digital images and entertaining stories. The name of the award winner is kept secret by the award committee, and the announcement remains a highlight of the year for the school's teachers.

Bryn Mawr and Gilman Schools participated in a joint Human Relations Day in 1984 to commemorate the 30th anniversary of the *Brown v. the Board of Education* decision, with presentations by speakers and discussions on "the future of opportunities for minorities at their schools, affirmative action, the ERA, and social Darwinism."[11]

The Cum Laude Society was established at Bryn Mawr in a convocation on April 4, 1984, when juniors in the top tenth and seniors in the top fifth of their classes were inducted.

Students participated in language immersion weekends in the early 1980s. Beginning in the 1984–1985 school-year, Latin would be required not only in eighth grade but also in seventh. Latin was offered at Bryn Mawr all through Upper School, and Greek was taught at Gilman.[12] While foreign language study had been an integral part of the Bryn Mawr curriculum since 1885, it had been widely eliminated or cut back in schools during the 1960s. The American Council on the Teaching of Foreign Languages was pleased to announce that the "return to basics" movement had brought about a resurgence in foreign language study. In a 1982 survey, the council found that nineteen percent of secondary students nationwide were enrolled in a foreign language course. The numbers were higher in metropolitan areas, such as Baltimore, where a greater influx of immigrants brought not just more languages, but an appreciation of their value in an increasingly global society.[13]

Charioteer Josh Shoemaker, Latin Day, 1986

On September 21, 1984, the entire school enjoyed a day of centennial festivities to launch the 100th academic year. September was declared to be Bryn Mawr School Month by both the mayor's and the governor's offices, while Senator Paul Sarbanes had a tribute to Bryn Mawr entered into the *Congressional Record.*

Barbara Chase recalled "students of all ages and the faculty–in a circle big enough to surround the grassy green fall fragrance of the Lower Field–[dancing] hand-in-hand at the end of a day that made us all realize how proud we are of our heritage, as well as our present."[14] That October, some of the approximately ninety Bryn Mawr School alumni, boys who had attended the primary school from the 1920s to the 1940s, had a reunion of their own in honor of the centennial.

The annual basketball game with St. Timothy's included archival photographs of games from the past and brought out a number of older alumnae to assist the faculty cheerleading team. In March, Bryn Mawr hosted "The Education of Girls: An Agenda for the Future," a conference that brought more than two hundred of the nation's leading figures in educational reform to the campus. The next month, in honor of the centennial, the Bryn Mawr Drama Club produced Edith Hamilton's translation of Euripides' The Trojan Women, under the direction of Josh Shoemaker. The Alumnae Centennial Gallery, a series of photographic displays highlighting different areas of professional pursuits of alumnae, first appeared on campus in the spring of 1985. The displays covered the fields of science and technology, followed by education in the fall. The displays continued through other career fields over the next several years as stories in Communiqué.[15]

The year concluded with the traditional Bryn Mawr Bazaar, beautifully transformed by Chair Jennie Lee Williams Fowlkes, Class of 1965, and her army of volunteers into a Victorian carnival, complete with a carousel, brass band, and racks full of costumes. More than five hundred alumnae representing Bryn Mawr classes from 1915 to 1984 participated in the Banner March; some three hundred followed Norma Simmons choreography in the alumnae dance. Gym Drill that day was truly spectacular, as approximately eight hundred students from Little School through Upper School took part, older girls partnering with younger girls for the dances. Yellow balloons were released by the juniors to honor the senior class, in place of the traditional throwing of daisies. The current and three former headmistresses were present, representing nearly a half century of Bryn Mawr School leadership.

The board revised the 1979 Master Plan during 1984 and 1985, noting that the school's priorities were to offer adequate compensation to attract the best faculty possible and to enhance the "geographic, ethnic, and economic diversity of the student body," which would require more funding for financial aid. Barbara Chase wrote that there were "a number of other areas and constituencies addressed by

Jennie Lee Williams Fowlkes, Class of 1965

the plan, but the two areas that stand out in my mind as the most important are our faculty and students. Without them, Bryn Mawr is 26 acres, 13 buildings and a history without a future." The board also updated the school's mission statement to reflect the great sense of community, diversity, and creativity they believed to be central to the mission of the school.[16] A newly released National Endowment of the Arts report about faculty attrition after the fourth year of teaching noted that the "most striking thing about the research is that when we look at the most effective schools . . . there is an altogether different pattern of faculty interaction. It is an extremely collaborative setting. The simple act of having teachers talk with one another makes a big difference in their attitude and performance."[17] Bryn Mawr had excelled at this for quite some time.

September of 1985 brought a revamped curriculum to the Middle School. After long and careful study, the faculty created a truly interdisciplinary program, giving each grade a specific topic of focus. Sixth grade would concentrate on American studies; for seventh grade it would be non-Western cross-cultural studies; and the eighth grade would combine the ancient and classical cultures with their second year of Latin. Cross-curricular planning would allow history and English classes to focus their reading and projects on a similar theme, which would also be brought into art and music classes. Whenever possible, field trips to museums, working farms, and other venues that could enrich the program were planned. A curriculum coordinator in each grade would ensure that the program ran smoothly and would seek out opportunities as they arose to enhance the studies.

In 1984, the Old Study Hall had been torn down to make way for a new Little School Building, allowing the quickly growing division to move out of its home in the Gordon Building Annex. In 1990, the Little School would expand into the back of the Old Gym to add the Infant/Toddler Center, with six faculty children and one grandchild among the first ten infants. Director Jean Hawley noted that "unlike

Centennial artwork created by Beth Barker White, Class of 1969

most non-public child care centers at that time, the Little School was open all year round and from 7:30 a.m. to 5:30 p.m. It's difficult to believe, but at that time the concept was fairly revolutionary."[18]

The former Little School building was renovated over the summer of 1985 to become the home for the music program for the Lower, Middle, and Upper Schools as well as Lower School arts; the building was renamed the Music and Arts Center, with rooms for both academic courses and choral and instrumental programs. Visiting alumnae would recognize the significance in this move as the building had housed the music program for years before the Little School had moved into it. At the same time, the volunteer-operated Bryn Mawrket merged with the bookstore in its present-day site near the cafeteria and gym.

Mini-Week, a January week-long program for the Middle School students of Bryn Mawr, Gilman, and Roland Park Country Schools, provided as many as one hundred and fifty different small classes and projects, including black and white photography, girls' water polo, the art of being a clown, computer music, aviation, film, and ceramics. A popular and exciting program, it required some five hundred volunteers to run and lasted for five years, from 1983 to 1988.

In February 1986, The Bryn Mawr School was one of the first group of thirteen public and private schools in the United States and Canada, and the only school in Maryland, to be named to the Associate School Network of the Coalition of Essential Schools. The coalition was cosponsored by NAIS and the National Association of Secondary School Principals and was formed to "promote substantive reform of secondary education." The coalition today describes associate schools as "places of powerful student learning where all students have the chance to reach their full potential. Diverse in size, population, and programmatic emphasis, Essential Schools serve K–12 students in urban, suburban, and rural communities."[19]

Also in 1986, at the suggestion of a recent senior class, forty hours of community service was a requirement for graduation, seven years before it was mandated for Maryland's public schools. The desire to give back to one's community had deep roots at Bryn Mawr, stretching back to the earliest days of box packing before 1900 and the Bryn Mawr School League's work beginning in 1910. The graduation requirement was also a direct result of the City Program and Senior Project that teacher Mimi Waxter had been instrumental in developing. The forty-hour requirement was soon changed to today's fifty hours of service.

The Centennial Campaign for faculty support, scholarship funds, and several school construction projects continued to raise funds well beyond the end of the celebrations. By the spring of 1987 the campaign had surpassed $3 million, and at the same time the Annual Giving fund reached record highs.[20] By June of 1986, the school could break ground on the greatly needed new auditorium and begin renovations to the kitchen and cafeteria. The Bryn Mawr community was invited in the winter of 1987 to "name a seat" by contributing $100 for a small plaque to be placed on the arm of one of the five hundred fixed, tiered seats in the auditorium. The Grandparents Fund spearheaded the campaign by raising the first half of the $50,000 needed to purchase the seats.[21] On April 9, 1987, Centennial Hall opened with the cutting of a giant ribbon that wrapped around the structure. What had been the stage of the former Elizabeth Thomas Auditorium was incorporated into the renovated cafeteria, while the rest of the former space became the Elizabeth Thomas Dance Studio, now used as athletic locker rooms. The first production held in the new, air-conditioned theater was the Lower School's performance of "Cinderella." Centennial Hall received an award from Preservation Maryland for the "design and construction of an appropriate new building extending a traditional campus design in 1987."[22]

Kira Isacoff, Class of 1997, and Barbara Chase with ceremonial scissors, April 9, 1987

Centennial Hall, 1987

After arranging for the sales of the home of the headmistress at 5613 Boxhill Lane and the Rosabelle Sinclair house at 5601 Woodlawn Road, Bryn Mawr purchased 5702 Stony Run, to provide more space for the social events and meetings that the position of headmistress required. The Chase family moved in during the summer of 1987.

Barbara Chase examined the curriculum of 1917 and found corollaries with the current academic program that would have made Bryn Mawr's founders proud. The VII Main (11th grade) in 1917 read *Hamlet, Prince of Denmark*, as did the 11th grade in 1984 (who also read *Death of a Salesman* and Sophocles' *Theban Plays*). In 1917 algebra was the most advanced math course, compared to Advanced Placement calculus in 1987. Tenth-grade science in 1917 consisted of "home economics with especial attention to hygiene," while Bryn Mawr girls of the 1980s could take biology or honors chemistry. As the school was headed into an accreditation and evaluation period with AIMS, as well as the Middle States Association of Colleges and Schools, Barbara Chase believed that Bryn Mawr, following in the footsteps of its first headmistress Edith Hamilton, would "strike a proper balance, as it always has, between the two extremes–finding and cherishing the golden mean."[23]

Rosanna Best and Lanaya Williams, Class of 1994, in Lower School

In October of 1984, the board of trustees, in a statement of protest against the practice of apartheid, voted to invest only in companies with operations in South Africa if they had signed the Sullivan Principles, which called for the respect of universal human rights. Three years later, the senior class of 1988 contributed $1,500 from their class treasury to help start Bryn Mawr's Independent School South African Education Program, which would allow two black South African students to study at Bryn Mawr for a transitional year between high school and an American college.[24] During the same time, independent schools and colleges were experiencing an increase in the enrollment of Asian American students, alongside a decline in some cases by as much as half, of the African American students on campus. The decline resulted from drastic cutbacks in funding assistance for financial aid and for programs that identified and supported gifted minority students. Continual struggling in the public school programs prepared fewer inner city school-children for independent school admissions.[25]

Bryn Mawr's participation as one of eight independent schools in NAIS' pilot Multicultural Assessment Project in 1988–1989 led to the creation of a Multicultural Committee on campus to organize dinners, speakers, and presentations.[26] The same year, Bryn Mawr founded the Baltimore Readers' Camp to assist disadvantaged rising fourth- and fifth-grade Baltimore city schoolchildren with their reading skills during the summers. Three years later, the Barbara Bush Foundation for Family Literacy awarded Bryn Mawr funding for "Readerdays," which would bring the campers' parents to the school on Saturdays to reinforce the skills learned and help provide parental support to the campers.[27]

Those who were watching "Good Morning America" on June 17, 1988, got an earful of enthusiastic Bryn Mawr students together with Barbara Chase shouting the show's name as an introduction to a segment about Baltimore. Charlie Gibson, the show's host and husband of former Middle School Director Arlene Gibson, shared several kind words about the school with the nation that morning.

In the early years, the center of campus was on Melrose Avenue, with the land near Belvedere Avenue, now Northern Parkway, filled with woods and not used by the school. At several times during financially difficult years, the board had considered selling some of that land or developing homes along it, but fortunately, never did. With a generous donation from A.V. Williams, a Bryn Mawr parent and grandparent, the Northern Parkway driveway was constructed in time for the opening of school in 1989, easing traffic congestion within the neighborhood around the school, and providing better traffic flow and more parking on campus.

Observations about the status of the school made by the 1990 Long-Range Planning Committee noted the caring environment and the strong academic program, particularly in the greater development of technology, math, and science curricula. Tri-school coordination was working successfully and provided an answer to the national trend of single-sex schools becoming coeducational. While annual donations to the school were on the rise, the small endowment remained an issue, as it did not provide sufficient income to cover the gap between tuition and operating expenses. The campus itself, while a beautiful setting, was aging; other than Centennial Hall there had been no major renovations or additions in the past decade, while enrollment had increased by twenty-five percent. The Long-Range Plan established several goals to be achieved by 1995, including keeping abreast of technological advancements and continuing to include the teaching of ethics in the curriculum; increasing ways to compensate faculty; considering the expansion of the kindergarten and transition program; increasing maintenance and formulating a building program for the future; and raising the endowment. The student body (excluding Little School) had grown from 542 to 675 in the last decade, while financial aid continued to improve from 11.4% to 15.6% in the same period. The plan called for providing 20% of students with financial aid in the future. The committee recommended a capital campaign to lower Bryn Mawr's dependency on tuition, covering 87% of the operating cost of the school in 1998–1990, much more than at other schools with larger endowments.[28] By the end of June 1991,

Girls reading together on Founders Day, 1991

the "Campaign for Bryn Mawr: A Tradition of Leadership" had collected or received pledges for $2.2 million toward the $6 million goal, of which $4 million would pay for campus improvements, including the new library and renovations to the Howell Building, a dance studio, and a lobby for Centennial Hall. The other $2 million would be added to the endowment to support both faculty and financial aid.[29] By the end of the campaign in 1994, the endowment stood at an all-time high of $7.7 million, about $10,000 per student in the Lower, Middle, and Upper Schools. In comparison, however, the endowment at girls' schools nationally was $15,243, and at all independent schools was nearly $22,000. Bryn Mawr was at capacity with 767 students (excluding the Little School) and would not be able to increase enrollment in the near future.[30]

Founders Day in October 1990 celebrated the anticipated construction of the new Upper School library, with older and younger students reading together and sharing their favorite books, poems, and stories. The Lower School embarked on a penny project to raise one million pennies by the end of the year to donate to the capital campaign.

Educational reforms had not reached the most troubled inner-city public schools by the end of the 1980s, and independent schools, businesses, and governments focused increased attention on their improvement. By the end of 1989, states had taken over entire school systems in New Jersey and California; baseball bat-wielding principal Joe Clark in Patterson, New Jersey, was profiled on the cover of *Time* magazine as he sought to take back his troubled high school from the violence of drugs and gangs. Baltimore's school systems were impoverished by the depletion of the tax base during the 1960s and 1970s flight of the middle class, both black and white, as well as the decline in population growth. Schools sought to be part of the solution, and on October 27, 1990, Bryn Mawr hosted "Independent Schools and At-risk Children: A National Conference" to examine ways that independent schools could be more creatively engaged in addressing the needs of at-risk children in their communities.

Although the cost of an independent school education had risen far beyond the cost-of-living increases over the last decade, enrollment continued to climb, but was coupled with greater requests for financial aid. The recession of 1991 would take its toll on endowments and fund-raising at a time when there were fewer students available to fill seats in high schools. As public schools were forced to lay off teachers and cut back on "non-essential" programs such as art, music, athletics, and programs for gifted students, applications to independent schools in 1991 were up as much as thirty-three percent in selected areas nationwide despite tuition costs.[31] At Bryn Mawr, Arts Council was made an equal partner to the Student Government and Athletic Associations the same year. A *Sun* editorial in September 1992 noted that while the cost of independent schools had climbed, they had already mastered many of the new reforms then being added to public high schools, such as required community service, and that they were "insulated" from the battery of testing and accountability that the public schools faced. The quality and value of independent schools were instead measured by "each semester's enrollment forms and tuition checks."[32]

The National Coalition of Girls' Schools (NCGS) was established in November of 1991 to promote girls' schools and girls' education. Bryn Mawr was one of the original fifty-six member boarding and day schools and housed the coalition's offices on its campus for several years. The coalition provided conferences, promotional information, and services in support of its member schools.

Barbara Landis Chase Dance Studio, 1990s

Completed in the summer of 1992 at a cost of $750,000, the new 2,500-square-foot dance studio and the 1,720-square-foot lobby of Centennial Hall incorporated glass, stone, steel, and stucco and continued the theme of covered walkways that connected buildings around campus. That winter, the buildings' designs by the architecture firm of Cho, Wilks & Benn (later Cho Benn Holback + Associates) received the Grand Design Award of the American Institute of Architects, which called it an "elegant solution to the problem posed" and "joyful, spare, light-filled and entirely appropriate to making a space for dance."[33] The dance studio was renamed for Barbara Landis Chase upon her leaving Bryn Mawr in 1994, while the theater lobby became the Mildred Natwick Lobby later that fall to commemorate the famous actress of stage and screen of the Class of 1924.

On April 30, 1993, the new Edith Hamilton Library addition was opened, with classrooms and a computer lab upstairs, and a new kindergarten-transition center downstairs. The renovated Howell Center housed the offices of admission and the headmistress. The twenty-five-year-old biology lab in Hardy was renovated the next summer as a gift of the parents of the Class of 1994. Parents of the Class of 1995 did the same for the chemistry lab.

Katie DiPentima and Patty Gerhardt, Class of 1994

When Barbara Landis Chase arrived at Bryn Mawr in 1980, there were 543 students in kindergarten through twelfth grade, and another 48 children in the Little School. In 1993, 757 students had enrolled in the school, with 218 children in the Little School; about one-quarter of the students represented minorities. Financial aid had risen from $94,611 to $790,774 during Barbara Chase's fourteen-year tenure, providing funds for 18.9 percent of students in the Lower, Middle, and Upper Schools.[34] Barbara Chase had made significant contributions to Bryn Mawr and brought the school to a place of national recognition for its outstanding academic, extracurricular, and community outreach programs, as well as an excellent faculty and student body. On her acceptance of the position as first female head of the 217-year-old Phillips Academy, Andover in 1994, she told *The Sun* that she felt a "sense of excitement about what lies ahead, but a real sense of loss about what I'm leaving behind. [Bryn Mawr] is a place characterized by such high energy and intelligence, and I will miss it."[35]

"As Barbara Chase once remarked, 'No one ever really leaves Bryn Mawr.' Bryn Mawr leaves an indelible imprint on your mind, your heart, and your soul."

Anne Edmunds Croker, Class of 1958, alumnae director 1982–1995, Communiqué, 1995

1924

Detail of the Campus Master Plan, 2001

Chapter Eight
BRYN MAWR IN THE TWENTY-FIRST CENTURY 1994–2010

Members of the Classes of 1994 and 1995

$\mathcal{E}$llanor "Bodie" Brizendine, former Bryn Mawr director of admission and financial aid, director of outreach programs, and teacher of English from 1981–1990, returned from San Francisco to serve as interim headmistress while the board sought a permanent replacement for Barbara Chase. On her arrival, she found a small box on her desk containing individually wrapped treasures that she would need for her job: "keys to the school and her office; the diploma-signing pen; book markers from the fourth grade International Bazaar to measure all my readings; little gold stars to reward the many; and a lovely turn-of-the-century 'good luck tablet' for note-taking." Wondering what would be appropriate to send to Barbara Chase in her new office in Andover, Bodie discovered a pair of Barbara's loafers tucked under the desk and sent them to her with the note, "These are hard to fill."[1]

To improve coordination among the three schools, Bryn Mawr, Gilman, and Roland Park Country shifted from forty- to seventy-minute class periods in September of 1994. This allowed for greater in-depth conversation in the classroom, as well as longer periods for activities and community service outside the classroom. A block of time in the middle of the day gave each campus the opportunity to schedule its own convocations and assemblies. The greatest benefit of the less frequent, but longer classes was that it allowed the students to prepare in greater depth and the teach-

Bodie Brizendine

ers to create more dynamic lessons with a variety of activities and projects. Teachers were excited about working in a less frantic format. As one teacher put it, "I'm walking on unscheduled air. It is a miracle—time to think, ask, breathe."[2]

The need to understand how children learn and what engages them best in the classroom has brought a variety of experts in the fields of child development to Bryn Mawr to talk with both faculty and parents over the years. In the spring of 1995, Bodie Brizendine brought author Dr. Michael Riera to campus. He suggested to parents that their role should be one of consultant or guide rather than manager, and he reminded teachers of the power that "self-discovery" brought to students, something that has long been a hallmark of a Bryn Mawr education.[3]

The dedication to Bodie Brizendine in the 1995 *Bryn Mawrtyr Supplement* noted: "Your prowess as an educator, your compassion as a friend, your spirit as a Mawrtian, and your quiet strength as a leader have taught us to seek these same qualities in ourselves and in our peers. We value the time we have had with you this year, and we will carry the values you taught us far beyond the halls of Bryn Mawr." Bodie Brizendine returned to California in the summer of 1995 to lead the Marin Academy in San Rafael.

Rebecca MacMillan Fox was chosen as Bryn Mawr's next headmistress in the spring of 1995. She came from "the distinctive coordinate college setting of Hobart and William Smith Colleges in Geneva, New York" where she had served as dean at the women's William Smith College since 1982. She had previously served as assistant dean of Bryn Mawr College for ten years, where she had also completed her bachelor's, master's, and doctoral degrees in French. Rebecca Fox was described by Richard T. Hale Jr., president of the board, as combining "intelligence, compassion, and vision with years of experience in all facets of women's education. She is absolutely first-rate."[4]

Rebecca MacMillan Fox

The peer education program, developed in 1994–1995 through funding from the Christopher O'Neil Memorial Fund, brought together Upper School students with fifth graders to focus on the topics of friendship, communication, tolerance, and stress, and to create positive coping skills through role-playing, games, and discussion. The program was developed by a team of Upper and Lower School teachers and counselors under the guidance of Dr. Charles Deutsch, an expert on alcohol education and director of the Harvard Health Education Project. It was designed to provide the younger students with tools to help them make good decisions when confronting social problems, with the goal of feeling secure about their choices in later years when confronted with drugs and alcohol. While both the younger and older students greatly enjoyed their time together and the project, the Upper School girls also gained new respect for their teachers, as they found how challenging it could be to work with a classroom full of bright and curious Bryn Mawr girls.[5] The following year, the fifth grade shared their compassion by crafting one thousand paper cranes to send to Hiroshima, Japan, as part of an international children's tribute to peace inspired by the children's book *Sadako and the Thousand Paper Cranes*, about a twelve-year-old victim of radiation from the atom bomb.

To understand better how Bryn Mawr prepared its students and what their experiences had been at the school, administrators began to meet individually with the Class of 1996 in a series of senior exit interviews. Today, these interviews, held after the academic program is completed, continue to provide the school with an important tool to evaluate the strengths and weaknesses of the student experience at Bryn Mawr, as well as to initiate the senior's transition from student to alumna.

Shara Khon Butler Duncan, Class of 1987, with her daughter Marina, Class of 2012

Shara Khon Butler Duncan, Class of 1987 and a teacher of Spanish since 1992, became Bryn Mawr's first diversity coordinator in the fall of 1996. As chair of the Community Alliance (formerly known as the Multicultural Committee), her goal was to strengthen Bryn Mawr's commitment to inclusiveness and to build a sense of community that recognized the diverse races, religions, socioeconomic backgrounds, and gender identities within it. A 1996 survey by the Sun found that minority enrollment at a number of independent schools, including Bryn Mawr, Gilman, and Roland Park Country, averaged about seventeen percent, surpassing minority enrollment at many of the desegregated public schools. Campus cultures began to reflect the growing diversity of their communities. Awareness clubs, celebration of diverse holidays, the addition of gospel choirs, and the inclusion of the writings of minority authors and global perspectives into the curriculum greatly expanded the viewpoint and experience in the schools and provided more opportunity for increased expression by community members.[6]

Children of the post–World War II baby boomers, the "baby boom echo" of the 1980s, were crowding the nation's schools by the mid-1990s, causing Maryland to cope with the "biggest crush of students in more than twenty years."[7] While enrollment in city schools was expected to peak in 1996, county schools were anticipating growing enrollment for years beyond that, particularly in middle and high schools, which might grow as much as thirty percent between 1992 and 2002. In 1994, AIMS reported steady increases in member school populations since 1989, while the archdiocese saw a ten percent rise in enrollment in just three years at Catholic schools, so that schools that had been about to close were suddenly thriving.[8] At Bryn Mawr, Director of Admission Bessie Cromwell (Speers), Class of 1982, told the Sun that applications were up twenty-eight percent from the year before and that many qualified applicants had to be put on the waiting list. Baltimore County added seven new magnet schools, doubling their number for the opening of school in the fall of 1994.[9] As the resources of the public schools strained to meet the quickly growing number of students, many parents who had left the cities for the free education of public schools in the suburbs now turned to the independent schools. Nationally, independent school enrollment in 1996 rose to eleven percent of the student population, with significant increases in metropolitan areas. Locally, parents cited the "lack of individual attention" and "overwhelmed teachers" in the public schools as significant factors that brought them to independent schools for the first time.[10] More of the families now applying did not come from a tradition of independent schools and were making greater financial sacrifices, often tapping their children's college funds to provide them with smaller class sizes and more rigorous curricula in preparation for college.[11] In the winter of 1997, every application to Bryn Mawr was read by eight different administrators, a daunting task given that applications were up 18.5 percent for all grades, and 49 percent for the sixth grade alone.[12] By the summer, the secretary of education projected that school enrollment nationwide would continue to climb each year through 2007.[13]

The surge in enrollment and demand for the latest in technology and facilities, coupled with exceptionally large gifts from alumni, families, and foundations, drove the independent schools to construct new buildings as they prepared for the next decade. No fewer than eight area schools, including Boys' Latin, Bryn Mawr, Garrison Forest, McDonogh, and Park were under construction, and many others were in the planning stages.[14] While some schools needed new arts facilities, classroom space, or athletic centers, advancements in the teaching of science and technology required more specialized buildings at many schools, including Bryn Mawr.[15]

Architect Marcel Breuer had not included dedicated space for science in his plans for the Lower School in the 1970s. For years, a science specialist wheeled a cart of materials from classroom to classroom, and five years later a room was redesigned for science, but it was still inadequate to serve the growing needs of the science curriculum. Lower School Director Peggy Bessent envisioned a new science building to mark the twenty-fifth anniversary in 1997 of the Lower School's buildings. As she explained to the board, science was important to the mission of Bryn Mawr, not only as an academic subject, but also because the nature of discovery in science encouraged risk-taking, making it "one of the very strongest ways we have to help girls develop or bolster their self-esteem." Plans called for an airy, light-filled structure nestled in the trees, where students could observe nature year-round from inside the classroom and outside on a large deck. Space for computers, experiments, and specimen collections would allow for long-term observation and analysis, and clusters of small work tables would permit groups of students to work on projects and to share ideas and tasks. On April 18, 1997, coinciding with National Science and Technology Week, the Lower School held the official inauguration of the 1,500-square-foot, $400,000 Science Center. With three walls of glass and a fourth exterior wall of stone, embedded with animal-themed bas relief tiles and a playground that would hold a DNA molecule climber made by sculptor Stan Edmister, it was, as one second-grader declared, "science heaven!"[16]

DNA molecule climber

Many independent schools in Baltimore were feeling the constraints of limited physical space, not just in their buildings, but on their athletic fields, as well. The land that they had each purchased in moving out to the country in the 1920s and 1930s was no longer adequate for the size of the student population and the variety of programs the schools offered in the twenty-first century. Bryn Mawr further expanded its campus holdings in December of 1998, when it purchased the Mount Washington Club on Cottonworth Avenue, just two miles from the Melrose campus. Mount Washington had been the home of the men's Wolfpack Lacrosse Club, and Bryn Mawr had rented the playing field from the association at this and the club's former site since Rosabelle Sinclair started girls' lacrosse at Bryn Mawr in 1926. With the purchase, the school acquired not only a much-needed and well-lit playing field, but also a clubhouse that provided locker rooms for home and visiting teams, a large parking lot, a full commercial kitchen, a meeting room and office, as well as a formal bar area and conference and ballroom space. The property would allow the school to hold parent meetings, student dances, retreats, phonathons, conferences, and seminars with colleagues from other schools and organizations. It would also provide rental income.[18]

Bryn Mawr's increasing commitment to environmental sustainability led to the choice of "green design" for the new Admission Cottage. It was the third Bryn Mawr building designed by the firm of Cho Benn Holback + Associates to be recognized by the American Institute of Architects. The Barbara Landis Chase Dance Studio had won the Grand Design Award in 1992, and the Lower School Science Center had received the same award in 1997. The Admission Cottage was built from wood recycled from the campus and environmentally sensitive materials, with both active and passive solar panels, a rain garden to minimize storm water runoff, floor tiles made from recycled glass from windshields and light bulbs, and countertops composed of the school's recycled paper and mail. It has been considered a leading model of green construction by many designers and ecologists who have come to the school to tour the building and to study its advanced design.

Bryn Mawr unveils the Governor's Green School banner, 1999

"Stewardship 2000: Bryn Mawr School's Environmental Initiative for the 21st Century" was launched at the groundbreaking of the Admission Cottage on June 11, 1998, as an outgrowth of the school's "long-standing commitment to discover new approaches to learning, thinking, and living that would promote a deeper understanding of our relationship with the environment."[19] Throughout the divisions, consideration for the environment had already been integrated into the curriculum, from Lower School nature, to sixth-grade earth sciences, to AP environmental science in Upper School, and through readings and studies outside of the sciences. Within a year, Bryn Mawr was designated as a Governor's Green School. At commencement in 2001, Rebecca Fox announced that the Julia Clayton Baker Chair in Environmental Stewardship had been established with a gift of one million dollars from the Baker family. Rebecca Fox noted that the chair would be central to "educating Bryn Mawr students to become agents of change and active builders and stewards of a sustainable, nurturing society."[20]

The Edith Hamilton Scholars Program, coordinated by history teacher Arna Margolis, was established in 1999 to provide inquisitive and talented seniors the opportunity, beyond grades and credits, to explore a subject of interest through independent study. The first applicants prepared proposals outlining their theses and method of research in the spring of their junior year in 1999 and submitted them to a committee of Upper School teachers and administrators. Students accepted to the program worked under the guidance of mentors who were experts in the chosen fields of study. The range of subjects explored by the scholars reflect their varied interests and include topics such as research and investigation into science, history, music, classics,

Arna Margolis with the first Edith Hamilton Scholars, Class of 2000: Betsy Wilson, Mamie Thant, Caroline Young, Rebecca Kiselewich, Ann Everton, Laura Perciasepe, and Meredith Monk

and language. Presentations to the school community over the years have included a wide range of media through formal papers, electronic presentations, original artwork, displays, and performances.

In 2000, Harkness Tables were brought to Bryn Mawr through the initiative of trustee Richard Berkeley, who realized they were a perfect fit for Bryn Mawr's instructional style. The large, oval tables created an inviting space for interactive, student-led discussion, and they were immediately successful in providing a new dynamic in English and history classes.

Middle School Director Dr. Jennifer Galambos leads a Harkness Table discussion, 2009

The increasing number of high school graduates who were eligible to apply to colleges and universities, growing availability of financial aid for lower-income applicants, and more aggressive international recruiting by universities combined to create a marked change in college admission patterns for independent schools during the 1990s. Daniel Golden reported in *The Wall Street Journal* on January 23, 2001, that "overall, private-school graduates constituted 32% of this year's freshman class at Harvard, compared with 44% in 1960." He pointed to an article from the Phillips

Academy, Andover student newspaper the year before that "noted wistfully that Harvard University, which admitted 69 of 74 applicants from Andover in 1950, took only 18 out of 89 a half-century later."[21] At the same time, increases in tuition at colleges, universities, and independent schools continued to rise above the rate of inflation, as institutions struggled with increasing costs of operating the physical plant and providing new technology, as well as maintaining adequate wages and benefits to attract and retain the best faculty and staff.

By the fall of 2000 and into the early months of 2001, it was clear that the economy was faltering for the first time in a decade, but significant indicators were mixed, leaving economists uncertain about what might happen. Unemployment, inflation, and interest rates were all low, but the general economy was growing at a much slower pace than before. At the same time, energy prices were once again soaring, companies were laying off employees and lowering their earnings reports, individual savings had dropped from seven percent to zero in ten years, and consumer confidence was reported to be as low as it had been during the 1991 recession.[22] For independent schools, a decline in annual revenues from endowment investments strained their abilities to maintain tuition costs at levels that would support between eighty and eighty-five percent of their operating budgets. Baltimore-area schools had been increasing tuition at about four to five percent each year over the past several years, but now would have to raise tuition significantly to continue to offer their existing programs. As the Bryn Mawr board deliberated the budget in the winter of 2001 for the next academic year, they were faced with further rising costs and declining revenues from investments, and they were holding to a specified spending rule of less than five percent of fair market value of the school's endowment. The board chose to increase tuition by 12.5 percent for the following year, opting for a very high level of confidence that the school would meet projected expenses, rather than increase tuition at a somewhat lower rate over the course of several years. More families were assisted with financial aid, and future increases returned to lower levels, comparable to those at neighboring schools. Four years later, NAIS President Patrick Bassett would note that nationwide, "tuition at top private schools climbed an inflation-adjusted 43% in the past decade," pointing to increased costs as well as greater demand from families for advanced curriculum and services.[23]

Rebecca Fox resigned from Bryn Mawr in April 2001, explaining in a letter to parents and alumnae that it had "become increasingly clear that the board and I disagree about fundamental matters of governance, policy and style of management. We therefore have concurred that Bryn Mawr should seek new leadership." Katy Dallam, Class of 1973, former teacher at Bryn Mawr, and on the faculty at Harford Day School, agreed to serve as interim headmistress while the board searched for Dr. Fox's replacement.

Jennie Lee Williams Fowlkes, Class of 1965, whose service and dedication to the school were unfaltering, was named a trustee emerita in the spring of 2001, making her the only permanent member of the board of trustees.

By 2000-2001, the school was outgrowing available space and several temporary structures were in use on campus. The architectural firm of Robert A. M. Stern was hired to develop a Campus Master Plan for future construction projects to be phased in over time at Bryn Mawr, incorporating the style of the current buildings while anticipating future needs. The school sought to "establish an overall vision and guiding instrument" for campus development for the next one hundred years.[24] Unveiled on October 24, 2001, the plan provided for several phases of construction and a reorganization of the buildings around a "Bryn Mawr Quadrangle," which would place the first new building at the north end of campus. The board had already approved a capital campaign to begin raising funds for both the endowment and the first building, and by April 30, 2002, had received more than $4.6 million in cash and pledges.

Katy Dallam

In the meantime, two small yet essential construction projects were undertaken. Bryn Mawr, Gilman, and Roland Park Country Schools installed two pedestrian bridges to connect the campuses after a Bryn Mawr student was struck by a car while crossing Northern Parkway on her way to class on another campus. Spanning Northern Parkway and Roland Avenue, the bridges were completed by spring of 2002, at a cost of more than $2 million, shared by the three schools.[25] In addition, the following fall, the transition class in the Lower School

Inaugurating the bridges, 2002

moved into its own newly constructed space, permitting expansion of the transition program between kindergarten and first grade.

On February 21, 2002, the board of trustees announced that Maureen E. Walsh, "an energetic and seasoned educator and administrator" had accepted the position as the ninth headmistress of Bryn Mawr. During her sixteen years at the Polytechnic Preparatory Country Day School in Brooklyn, New York, she had served as director of admission and financial aid, assistant head, and then head of the new Poly Prep Lower School, located several miles from the main campus, and in many ways a school standing on its own. Maureen Walsh earned her undergraduate degree in American studies from Wesleyan University and her graduate degree in educational administration from Columbia University. She also had taught at the Groton School and Phillips Academy, and she had served as assistant director of admission at Williams College.[26] As she arrived on the Bryn Mawr campus, new heads of schools recently had been, or were being, welcomed locally at Friends, Gilman, Oldfields, St. Paul's School for Girls, and St. Timothy's Schools.

One of Maureen Walsh's top priorities was to see that the first phase of the Campus Master Plan could begin as soon as possible to ease the crowding on campus. Construction of the North Building would provide much-needed classroom space, and the removal of the temporary classroom buildings would increase available parking and improve the look of the campus. After several years of planning and fundraising, the groundbreaking ceremony kicked off the Bazaar on Saturday, May 7, 2005, and the North Building was completed in September 2006. The three-story, 28,500-square-foot building was constructed with the same stone from the Butler quarry in Pennsylvania used in the older campus buildings. Inside, two science labs, a language lab, a computer lab, a performing arts studio, numerous large classrooms with Harkness Tables, a faculty room, and administrative offices give ample room for academic programs. A large lobby provides space for numerous activities and events, while terraces permit classes and functions to be held outside seasonally.

The "Bryn Mawr. *Always*" campaign, announced in October of 2006 with a goal of $25 million, well surpassed that figure. One-half of the funds raised would go to the endowment, in support of financial aid, faculty compensation, and to unrestricted funds "to respond to immediate opportunities in every area, from the cur-

Maureen E. Walsh

riculum to student activities."[28] In recognition of her dedication and service to the school, and in thanks for her chairmanship of the "Bryn Mawr. *Always*" campaign, Trustee Ann Hankin was made an honorary alumna in 2007.

For years, Bryn Mawr students have enjoyed group exchanges with schools in France, Germany, and Spain. Bryn Mawr's reputation led schools in other nations to inquire into establishing formal exchange programs for individual students. Under Maureen Walsh's conviction of the value of such a program, Bryn Mawr sophomores and juniors now may apply to spend a month living with a host family or in a boarding school and attending school in West Sussex, England; Prague in the Czech Republic; Cape Town, South Africa; and the Gold Coast in Australia, and to host a student in return. Erin Munoz, diversity coordinator and director of global programs, also seeks out community service projects abroad for Bryn Mawr students to further expand their understanding of the world as a whole. In 2010, students can fulfill their Community Service Learning requirement working with orphans in the Dominican Republic.

Headmistress Maureen E. Walsh, Past Chair, Board of Trustees, Georgia D. Smith, Class of 1972; and Chair, Board of Trustees Chair and Honorary Alumna Ann D. Hankin

A long-awaited renovation of the Lower School had teachers packing their classrooms into boxes as school closed for the summer in June of 2009. Demolition teams held their hammers during the graduation ceremonies just a few days later, and as the last student left campus the Lower School buildings' roofs came off, inner walls were torn out, and a beautifully updated and air-conditioned series of buildings was ready just weeks later for school in the fall. Marcel Breuer's open classroom design was made more efficient for teaching in the twenty-first century, with a series of beautiful clerestory windows pouring natural light into the newly named Peggy Bessent Library. In May 2010, the United States Green Building Council awarded LEED (Leadership in Energy and Environmental Design) certification for the building, recognizing that appropriate environmental choices had been made during the renovation. Administrators took this opportunity to reconsider the placement of the fifth grade in the Lower School in the 1970s when the Main School was divided into the Middle and Upper schools. The academic and emotional development of fifth-grade students in the twenty-first century as compared to fifty years earlier warranted a change. Renovations to the music and art buildings provided the fifth grade with its own physical space and a sense of independence to transition from the Lower school to the Middle school.

Peggy Bessent Library, Lower School, dedicated 2010

"Vision 2020" was designed as a planning instrument by the board to "develop a vision of the school in 2020 and to identify the initial steps toward making that vision a reality." The document touched on goals about students, teachers, global learning, community responsibility and service, environmental sustainability, alumnae relations, and the campus in the twenty-first century.

In preparation for reaccreditation by the Association of Independent Maryland Schools and the Middle States Association of Colleges and Schools in 2009, each member of the faculty and staff worked on one of fourteen committees overseen by Associate Headmistress Peggy Bessent and English teacher Peter Metsopoulos. Over the course of a year of self-study, committees gathered and analyzed information and examined every aspect of the school's operations following the guidelines established by the associations. A visiting committee then spent several days surveying the school and asking questions, comparing the self-study report with its observations, and found that Bryn Mawr met the mission it set for itself, and did so quite well. As the committee noted in its final report: "After reading the self-study we came to campus expecting a great school and found something much more profound. We prepared to see a well-run school with excellent programs and a talented faculty, a very strong curriculum, excited and exciting students, and a rich sense of tradition and place. In point of fact, we found that Bryn Mawr is a truly special school whose clear sense of its history and provenance guides it still today. . . the committee saw clearly that students and faculty embody the desire to live 'considered and consequential lives.' The 'demands and delights of learning' are visible in the classroom, on the athletic field and the stage, and in the way that the girls go about their daily responsibilities. Bryn Mawr girls experience the latter and aspire to the former with a determination and fierceness that is rare and worthy of emulation. The committee applauds Bryn Mawr's thoughtful and very successful efforts to continuously connect the present to the past kindling a spark of self-efficacy in young women that carries them to their future."

Anna Loup, Class of 2010, found that Bryn Mawr's mission statement also resonated with the alumnae she interviewed for her Edith Hamilton Scholar's project. Throughout her senior year, Anna interviewed Bryn Mawr graduates whose experience with the school spanned more than 80 years. As she shared today's mission statement with them, the alumnae each found relevance in the way that the school described itself for the twenty-first century with the school they knew. She found that "we, as Bryn Mawr students and alumnae, have been given the tools to live a life that 'respects diversity,' 'has a sense of responsibility to the broader community,' 'is resilient in the face of complexity, ambiguity, and change,' and, finally, is 'considered and consequential.' Having only recently graduated, I am now beginning to take on a new part of my journey, the one where I begin to define my considered and consequential life. The years girls spend at Bryn Mawr are times when the ideals are taught to students through curriculum and the examples of teachers.

However, the real test of a Bryn Mawr education begins after graduation . . . I think that the ideals of Bryn Mawr are just as strong as the image of the portico full of students on the first day of school, the decorations of the senior room, the Gym Drill sashes, and the pink flowers that fall from the cherry blossom trees every spring."

Bryn Mawr retains a strong bond to the ideals of the school's founders and the educational philosophy of Edith Hamilton. Dedicated to excellence in the education of girls and young women, cognizant of their far-reaching abilities and desire for achievement, and adept at supporting and nurturing their interests and talents, Bryn Mawr continues to be a leader in girls' education in the twenty-first century.

"May you be nourished by your dreams, guided by your ideals, and may your path in life be one of peace and of striving for the greater good."

Maureen E. Walsh, 2003 Valedictory Address in Communiqué

Student Government Association, 1923

The Bryn Mawr School founders were committed to providing a rigorous education for girls, as well as the development of the skills and self-confidence required to become leaders in their communities. The school has continued this strong tradition of students taking active and responsible roles by providing opportunities for leadership on campus, as well as through formal educational programs. Beginning with the Values Program in Lower School, students learn to treat others respectfully and with dignity, and experience from a young age the satisfaction of being supportive of and helpful to their peers. Bryn Mawr students learn to become confident and compassionate, and to respect differing ideas and opinions. They are encouraged to think beyond their own needs and to consider the school community as well as the world around them, and to recognize not only that they are capable of effecting change, but also that they have a responsibility to be active members of their community. They are encouraged to explore ideas that they are passionate about and find ways to support them through independent study, community service, and leadership roles at school.

Bryn Mawr provides rich opportunities for student leadership, beginning with the Lower School Student Council, through the leadership of a wide variety of clubs and organizations in Middle and Upper Schools, to the elected officers of the Upper School-wide organizations: Arts Council, Athletic Association, Community Alliance for Everyone, Community Service Learning, and Student Government Association. Each of these organizations serves a vital role in the daily life and management of the school.

Student Government Association

The first student government organization in the United States was established at Bryn Mawr College in 1892, while Edith Hamilton was a student there.[1] Believing that "it was much better for the individual development and for the spirit of the school for girls to work out their own system of government," Hamilton initiated a similar organization at The Bryn Mawr School soon after becoming headmistress in 1896.[2] In 1907, when the seniors were given their own study room, they created the school's first formal system of government, monitoring the hallways and keeping order while the entire student body moved silently up and down the enormous stairways. By 1911, proctors carried small notebooks hanging from golden cords on their left shoulders to record students' infractions, which were read aloud every other week to the entire school. Three marks were given for speaking in the halls, two for speaking in the library, and one for causing a disturbance. Any student who accumulated ten marks in two weeks would be required to take an extra gym class. Girls who had served three times wore two gold stripes on their sleeves as honor proctors, and earned the right to arrive late at school if they did not have a first period class, as well as leave school during a study period.[3] A formal constitution was written in the early 1920s, and in 1927 the system was revised to include participation by the students from second through twelfth grades, as well as elected leaders of school organizations and a member of the faculty.

Kelly Newman, Class of 2009, signing the honor statement in September, 2008

Adjustments and refinements were made over the years, but in 1958 a new system emphasizing a "high principle of honor by placing the responsibility of government on every girl in the school" reinvigorated the SGA.[4] The previous system of demerits was replaced with an honor system by vote of the entire Main School student body.

After discussing the merits and weaknesses of constitutions and government in class, the students drafted a new SGA constitution in 1964, reducing ten pages of rules to two, and placing the heads of all the clubs and school organizations on the Student Council. Ann Anderson, Class of 1964 and president of the Self-Government Association, wrote in the 1965 *Winter Bulletin* that the purpose of the SGA in the past had been to "curtail general freedom so that each individual may have complete enjoyment of [her] freedom" by establishing rules of conduct for the school community. In 1964, students felt that the "new Self-Government Association must move on to cover the second duty of government: helping a student to take advantage of her freedom" by providing opportunities through volunteer work to "take active responsibility in the school and in the Baltimore community."[5] SGA surveyed student activity in the community in 1968, and found that of 254 girls in grades seven through twelve, 61 were actively volunteering on their own, but 174 others wanted to participate in community service.[6] Over the next three decades, SGA assisted students by organizing opportunities to contribute to and participate in meaningful community service projects.

By 1998, Community Service Learning (CSL) was formally established as a separate organization to meet the school's mission of preparing students "to become responsible and confident participants in the world." Susan Solberg, then dean of students and now director of the Upper School, further noted that CSL would provide students with "the tools to interpret their lives and our society, the skills to effect change, and the confidence to believe that their work and ideas matter."[7]

Dean of Students Jeanette Budzik, Merve Gurakar, and Julia Clemens, Classes of 2010 and 2012, preparing for the "Hope for Haiti" fund-raising fair, 2010

Maureen Walsh and Little School Director Pat Sheridan with Little and Lower School students and faculty helping with the Buddy Packs project, 2005

Athletic Association (AA) also has deep roots at Bryn Mawr and was first mentioned in the May 1902 Bryn Mawrtyr, as the girls were trying to determine how much they should pay in dues to support their activities to encourage school spirit. Athletic Association arranged for the students to attend the annual basketball game against St. Timothy's, writing songs and cheers, and organizing the tea and celebrations before and after the game. To raise both the quality of play and school spirit, Athletic Association placed students onto intramural teams to play against each other and held annual games between the classes. As new sports were introduced at school, AA was responsible for the upkeep of the locker room and the requisite uniforms and equipment. Under Rosabelle Sinclair, AA often chose the varsity team players and arranged games with other schools. Today, Athletic Association continues to encourage school spirit, organizing Spirit Day events throughout the year and supporting the wide variety of athletic teams.

The Morgan State University Marching Band helps celebrate Spirit Day, 1999

Middle School Camera Club, 1955

Artistic activity outside the classroom had thrived through the years at Bryn Mawr through the Tuesday drawing class, Art Club, Stage Club, Photography Club, and other similar organizations and activities. In 1991, Arts Council was created as an equal partner in student leadership with Athletic Association and Student Government, to promote the arts at school and to create an opportunity for the school's fine and performing artists to engage further with the community. Arts Day, in 1995, brought together the tri-coordinate schools to celebrate and explore the arts through fifty-two different workshops held throughout the day in dance, bookbinding, bead and candle making, and improvisation, among many others. Alongside a wide array of events and activities that it sponsors, Arts Council hosts coffeehouses as well as an annual "Battle of the Bands" for student musical groups to perform.

Community Alliance For Everyone (CAFÉ) sought to "move Bryn Mawr beyond tolerance and into acceptance" of full diversity.[8] Through a variety of activities, including potluck dinners and mix-it-up lunches, CAFÉ seeks to bring the entire school community closer together.

Bryn Mawr reserves the last period of each day for meetings of these organizations as well as for the many clubs, activities, and publications of the school. In 2009–2010, there were as many as fifty student clubs and activities in the Upper School, each run by students elected by members or selected by the advisor. Upper School clubs of an academic nature, such as Model United Nations, "It's Academic," and Princeton Model Congress are so popular that members must be selected from among applicants. Several clubs center on community service and global understanding, such as Amnesty International, Make a Difference, Mission S.O.S., Operation Smile, and Vox Mundi. Other clubs focus on a particular interest, such as AIDS Awareness, Black Student Union, Gay Straight Alliance, Jewish Student Association, Muslim Student Association, the Young Democrats, and the Young Republicans Clubs, as well as language-oriented clubs for French, German, and Spanish. Each of these groups provides students with an opportunity to support a cause or explore a topic in greater depth, to educate and involve their classmates, to share their interests and concerns with other like-minded club members, and to take on a leadership role. The Middle School also hosts a wide variety of clubs run by faculty advisors, which vary each semester according to student and faculty interest.

The 2003–2004 "It's Academic" team members Marjorie Folie, Class of 2006, Ali Lapinsky, Class of 2004, and Stasia Badder, Class of 2006, with Upper School Director Susan Solberg and coach Julien Meyer

FINE & PERFORMING ARTS

Watercolor of Bryn Mawr students, circa 1960s, artist unknown

Mary Elizabeth Garrett was a connoisseur of fine art, with an impressive collection that she occasionally made available for public viewing in the gallery of her Mt. Vernon Place mansion. To enhance their academic studies and cultivate their appreciation of the fine arts, she surrounded the students at Bryn Mawr with expensive replicas of sculpture, paintings, and drawings that she had shipped from Europe. She also made sure that the art studio, tucked under the roof of the Cathedral Street building, provided natural light through skylights. The early emphasis on drawing, one of the original required subjects of The Bryn Mawr School, was also pragmatic; young women could earn a good living and contribute to the sciences by drawing medical or natural specimens, as well as become fine artists. The younger students drew specimens in their science classes, while the older girls sketched architectural fragments and plaster statuary in the school, as well as still life studies, portraits, and the scenery outside the windows of the art studio. At the first graduation, in 1893, a prize in drawing was awarded alongside the college scholarships and the athletic award. Every student attended art class two mornings a week, while those who were truly talented and interested were invited back to the school on Tuesday afternoons to sketch with Gabrielle de Veaux Clements, a noted Philadelphia artist who taught at Bryn Mawr from 1895 to 1911. While at the school, she designed and created murals throughout the region, including those for the Trinity Episcopal Church in Towson, and she etched scenes of The Bryn Mawr School and of Baltimore. After Mary Elizabeth Garrett's death in 1915, M. Carey Thomas commissioned Clements to make two copies of John Singer Sargent's portrait of Miss Garrett at Johns Hopkins University. One copy resides at Bryn Mawr College, while the other was placed above the first landing of the Cathedral Street building and was moved to the Garrett Building after its completion in 1933. M. Carey Thomas wrote the memorial inscription on the bronze plaque underneath.

Under Miss Clements' guidance, the artists of the school created the scenery for school plays, illustrations for the *Bryn Mawrtyr*, and posters and brochures for school events.[1] Miss Clements held frequent art shows and displays of student artwork in the school.

In the 1920s, the students were encouraged by art instructors Margaret Law and Gertrude Stanwood to draw whatever they wanted, contrary to common practice, and to use their artwork to express themselves in other classes. They drew pictures in their English and history notebooks and illustrated stories that they were reading in pencil, charcoal, and crayon. They also modeled figures in clay. This freedom of

Charlotte Mills

Watercolor by Janet T. Howell, Class of 1906, of John Keats' poem "To Autumn"

Lower School papier-mâché art project

expression was so novel at the time that the *Sunday Sun* ran a full-page article on June 7, 1925, entitled "Girls at Bryn Mawr School Paint Original Pictures," which encouraged other Baltimore children to do the same at home.[2]

Bryn Mawr students were often taken to the Walters Art Gallery to study the work of a particular artist, genre, or movement, incorporating what they learned into their work. They were among the first visitors to the Baltimore Museum of Art when it opened on February 23, 1923, in Mary Elizabeth Garrett's former mansion. Many Bryn Mawr School families and faculty helped to raise funds in support of the city's million-dollar loan to establish a new museum facility on four acres of land donated by Johns Hopkins University in 1924.[3]

From 1935 to 1960, Eleanor Graham taught Bryn Mawr girls "to observe [the] world and appreciate relationships within the whole . . . to have the experience of experimenting with a large variety of materials to be used in the creative process of self-expression."[4] In the 1930s and 1940s, students were required to take art classes from preschool through Main IV, with electives available in the afternoon in the Upper School. They also continued to use their art skills in other classes, illustrating the prose in their ballad books for English class, similar to medieval manuscripts, and embellishing their history and science notebooks. Later years brought ceramics kilns, photographic darkrooms, and greater space in the studio for work in collages, stained glass, and self-portraits in both two and three dimensions.

The Upper School Art Club, which created the Bazaar program covers on its own printing press made from a clothes wringer in 1962, was replaced in the fall of 1966 by a partially accredited studio class taught by Janice Proctor.[5] Mrs. Proctor emphasized creativity over technical skill and was credited by many of her former students for helping them discover a lifelong interest in art.

Bryn Mawr students today enjoy a wide array of art media in a program that continues to emphasize cross-curricular studies. Lower School students explore printmaking, drawing, painting, watercolor, sculpture, weaving, and more, and their artwork is frequently displayed throughout campus alongside the work of the older girls. Art teachers Charlotte Armstead and Diane Margiotta have taught the fine arts in the Middle and Upper Schools, respectively, since 1984, each guiding her students through a variety of media, including computer artwork, and bringing guest artists to campus to discuss their art and work with the girls. Additional instructors in the Upper School provide instruction in photography, drawing, and painting.

Above: Janice Proctor retired in 1977 after teaching art at Bryn Mawr for 24 years, the last seventeen of which she directed the department

Top Left: Middle School art teacher Charlotte Armstead with Nia Ebrahim, Class of 2016, and Erin Moore, Class of 2014

Bottom Left: Upper School art teacher Diane Margiotta with Karen Chen, Class of 2013

MUSIC AT BRYN MAWR

While drawing and elocution were considered essential to the academic program in 1885, there was no formal music instruction in the school until the early 1920s. After several years of occasional programs taught by a Bryn Mawr College lecturer, Elizabeth Robinson was hired in 1922 and established the first Glee Club, for which forty students were accepted after auditions. A separate choir was created with half the members to sing daily at morning prayers. Miss Robinson left at the end of the year, and the school then hired Elizabeth Merriam, who would lead music instruc-

Glee Club, 1923

tion at Bryn Mawr for forty years. Miss Merriam taught all of the singing in school, which was required through Main III, and she led the Glee Club and Junior Glee Club, which she added in 1926. She also introduced Gilbert and Sullivan operettas, which would eventually alternate with the Dramatic Club play every other year. Sandra Frey Hawthorne, Class of 1952, recalled that Miss Merriam introduced the students "to every kind of music–South American, African, Hispanic, and French folk music, French and Italian Bel Canto, Gilbert and Sullivan, everything." The Bryn Mawr Glee Club began singing with Gilman and Roland Park Country Schools as early as March 1940, in a concert featuring the music of Bach and Mozart, as well as from "Hansel and Gretel" and "The Mikado."

The Glee Club chose to use the proceeds of its 1952 performance of Gilbert and Sullivan's *Patience* to purchase a set of twenty-five handbells for the school. The handbells, which ranged chromatically across two octaves, were made to order from the Whitechapel Bell Foundry of London (makers of Big Ben and the Liberty Bell) and arrived in January 1955. Played at Christmas celebrations, concerts, and weekly practice sessions by many Bryn Mawr students over the last fifty-five years, they have been restored and some replaced by Middle School teacher and handbell choir director, Fred Rheinhardt, who currently directs Ex Solo, In Aere, and In Aura in the Middle School, and Ad Solem in the Upper School.

From left to right: Chinyere "ChiChi" Amanze, Renn Andrews, Celia Bell, Fred Rheinhardt, Theo Matthai, and Fairleigh Barnes

In 1956, a select choir was chosen from the members of the Glee Club and later renamed the Cambrian Choir. Performing for the first time at the Goucher Singing Workshop, the choir sang chamber music and the traditional songs of the Christmas Pageant.[6] On April 30, 1982, Bryn Mawr's Day of Art and Music, the Cambrian Choir sang alongside the new "Day's Eye Singing Group," which would then replace it that year as the select chorus of the junior and senior classes.[7]

The Junior Glee Club, active since 1926, continued for seventh- and eighth-grade singers as the Canterbury Choir in the fall of 1972, under the lead of Elizabeth Houston, who also directed the Bell Choir.[8]

In the fall of 1975, as membership in activities was declining so rapidly that the Christmas Pageant might not be staged, the school required that every Middle and Upper School student join at least one afternoon organization which met weekly. The choices available at the time were Canterbury or Cambrian Choir, Drama Club, ceramics, jewelry making, photography, The *Quill*, and field hockey and badminton squads. *Melange*, Symposium, and Cinema Club did not meet frequently enough to meet this new requirement.[9] During the 1990s, vocal groups in the Upper School included Camerata, Dayseye, and the choir.

Music in the Lower School curriculum uses the Orff-Schulwerk approach to put instruments, including xylophones, drums, and recorders, into the hands of children to let them express themselves even before they can read music. Student musical instruction in Middle School includes theory, composition, and criticism, and all sixth graders perform in the Sixth-Grade Chorus. Middle School students may join a string ensemble or one of the handbell choirs, or the seventh- and eighth-grade choral ensemble, Sumus Deae. In Upper School, students in the ninth, tenth, and eleventh grades may join Camerata, while Dayseye continues as the auditioned choir for juniors and seniors, with frequent off-campus concerts. Both singing groups count as an academic subject in a participant's schedule as they meet during the day. String Ensemble and the handbell choir, Ad Solem, are also available for musically inclined students. Private lessons are offered at Bryn Mawr in a variety of instruments as well as voice. Bryn Mawr's musical instructors work with other faculty on projects such as music and math discovery and adapt and compose their own work for the students.

Middle School Music Instructor Ken Whitley leads the Class of 2016 in the Sixth-Grade Chorus during the Winter Concert, 2009–2010

Dayseye sings the National Anthem before an Orioles Game at Camden Yards, 2005

DRAMA

In an era when the study of elocution and literature was a hallmark of a girl's life, plays, skits, and recitations were a central element of a Victorian girls' educational and recreational experience. Dramatic arts always have been incorporated into the curriculum and the co-curricular programs at Bryn Mawr. Students presented plays for other classes as part of programs to raise funds for charities or for the school and to celebrate the significant events of the school year, such as the senior banquet. From the earliest days at Cathedral Street until the construction of a dedicated auditorium in Centennial Hall, the school struggled to rehearse and prepare a stage for a play on the same floor that was used for physical education and sports. Letters in the archives collection chronicle the cost and inconvenience of bringing stage sets from storage in the barns at Montebello to the Cathedral Street building for the annual class plays.

In March of 1893, *The Sun* reported that the young men in The Bryn Mawr School's Dramatic Club presentation of a three-act comedy, "A Scrap of Paper," could not have been "more attractive and dapper."[10] Actually, until 1948 the "men" on the stage at Bryn Mawr were schoolgirls in costume, but in the early years propriety would require that they wear petticoats and eventually bloomers instead of pants under their jackets and coats.[11]

The Myth of Proserpine, 1897

Designing and fabricating sets and costumes involved all the students of the Main School and the art instructors, who would help them create "paper blossoms, white and pink, fastened by the hundreds to bare branches, and tall fox-gloves of the same material" for plays such as the April 1910 presentation of *A Midsummer Night's Dream* for the benefit of the Bryn Mawr School League.[12] The school was coached for *Midsummer* by Mr. Samuel King, "teacher of elocution and dramatics at Harvard, Columbia and Bryn Mawr College," and after its success, the girls reestablished the Dramatic Club.[13]

Candles used to illuminate the stage were replaced by electric lights after the curtain caught fire between the third and fourth acts of Main III's production of "The Rose of Alhambra" in 1911. The fire was quickly put out by fathers in the audience.[14] The 1917 production of "The Romancers" may have been overshadowed by the admission of boys to the audience. The students had decided

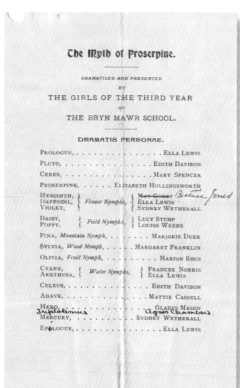

The Myth of Proserpine.

DRAMATISED AND PRESENTED
BY
THE GIRLS OF THE THIRD YEAR
OF
THE BRYN MAWR SCHOOL.

DRAMATIS PERSONAE.

PROLOGUE, ... ELLA LEWIS
PLUTO, ... EDITH DAVISON
CERES, ... MARY SPENCER
PROSERPINE, ... ELIZABETH HOLLINGSWORTH
HYACINTH, } Flower Nymphs, { MAY GOSBY *Beatrice Jones*
DAFFODIL, } { ELLA LEWIS
VIOLET, } { SYDNEY WETHERALL
DAISY, } Field Nymphs, { LUCY STUMP
POPPY, } { LOUISE WEEKS
PINA, Mountain Nymph, ... MARJORIE DUER
SYLVIA, Wood Nymph, ... MARGARET FRANKLIN
OLIVIA, Fruit Nymph, ... MARION ROUS
CYANE, } Water Nymphs, { FRANCES NORRIS
ARETHUSA, } { ELLA LEWIS
CELEUS, ... EDITH DAVISON
AGAVE, ... MATTIE CASSELL
HERO, ... GLADYS MASON
Triptolemus *Agnes Chambers*
MERCURY, ... SYDNEY WETHERALL
EPILOGUE, ... ELLA LEWIS

to give the proceeds to aid the Belgians, suffering starvation due to the war, and to help raise more funds the faculty agreed that boys could buy tickets, joining a Bryn Mawr School audience for the very first time. Rather than showing off for the boys, the girls felt they were taking a risk by appearing in their "moustaches, trousers, and wigs; in short, looking like nothing anyone ever saw before! Who knows how many hearts we may have lost that night!"[15]

The 1924 production of "A Kiss for Cinderella" sold out two nights' worth of tickets, raising nearly a thousand dollars for the scholarship fund and beginning the tradition of presenting each play on two separate occasions.[16]

Mary Guion Williams Griepenkerl, Class of 1932, returned to Bryn Mawr to teach English and dramatics and led the Dramatic and Stage Clubs from 1939 to

BRYN MAWR GIRLS PRESENT PLAY AT SCHOOL

Twenty-nine Members of Dramatic Club Appear in "A Kiss For Cinderella" Before Large Crowd in Auditorium

1982. Under her direction, so many students wanted to perform in Dramatic Club that members who had been in a play were not eligible to perform in the small skits that she arranged for assemblies, to ensure that everyone had a chance to perform on stage.[17] Many students, such as Corty Banks Fengler, Class of 1960, remember that her "attention to the details of inflection, projection and demeanor affected generations of Bryn Mawr girls" and gave them the ability to speak in public.[18]

Gilbert and Sullivan's Pirates of Penzance, 1956

March 30 and 31, 1928, marked the first joint production of the Dramatic and Glee Clubs as fifty students took the stage in "The Gondoliers." Annual spring plays then alternated each year between a drama and a musical.[19]

Gilman boys joined the Dramatic Club on Bryn Mawr's stage on January 10 and 11, 1952, for productions of "The Old Lady Shows Her Medals" and "Hands Across the Sea." It was also the first time that Stage Club worked jointly with Dramatics.[20] Bryn Mawr girls today continue to share the stage with Gilman as well as Boys' Latin.

Play acting and performance occurs often in Bryn Mawr classrooms, from skits in language classes to the production of videos in group projects in history class. In the Lower School, the third-grade Greek mythology studies culminate in the production of a mythological play that the students have written. Drama courses are added in the Middle School curriculum, where sixth graders explore dramatic expression, enacting short scenes and staging a production at the end of the year. Eighth graders learn movement and breathing skills and write and perform monologues, skills that support the five-minute convocation they will present with the guidance of their English teacher. Their English studies include reading Edith Hamilton's

Merve Gurakar presenting her Senior Convocation, 2010

Mythology, and a performance of a Greek myth play. Upper School students have courses in film studies, acting, and stagecraft available to them, as well as the opportunity to direct their own work. Annually, there are two large-scale productions with Gilman for which students may audition, as well as Stage Club, through which they learn about lighting, costumes, and set design and construction.

Julia Denick Class of 2011 and Meghan Stanton Class of 2010 in Oliver!

After thirty-four years of teaching Bryn Mawr students dramatics, English, and public speaking, Josh Shoemaker retired in 2010. He taught much more than that. As Kris Schaffner, Class of 1993 said of him, "He never once expressed doubt. On the contrary, he operated with absolute generosity and faith, and all of his students benefited from his hope, his courage, and his trust in us. Because he believed so deeply in all of us . . . and because he gave us the opportunity to play and risk and grow. . . we believed in ourselves, no matter the costume or scene or song. I guess that's part of what being connected to an extraordinary experience means. You never even notice that you are in the presence of outstanding teaching because—incredibly—you are used to it."

Over the years, Bryn Mawr women have taken the theatrical talents they learned and refined at the school on to the professional and amateur stage, including actresses Mildred Natwick and Eleanor Phelps of the Class of 1924 and Bess Armstrong, Class of 1971. Others, such as Xan Parker and Elizabeth Holder of the Class of 1988 have gone into the production of films, and Margo Lion of the Class of 1962, is an award-winning Broadway producer.

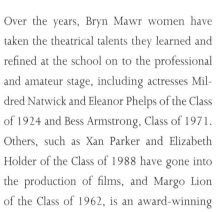

Upper left, Carol Worthington, Class of 1937, Marnie Bartlett, Class of 1938, and Scottie Fitzgerald, Class of 1939, daughter of F. Scott Fitzgerald, in Pride and Prejudice, 1935; Upper right, Mildred Natwick, Class of 1924; Bottom left and right, Bess Armstrong, Class of 1971, talking with students in Centennial Hall and in a performance at Center Stage as Joan of Arc

DANCE

Middle and Upper School dance at Bryn Mawr was taught until recently by the athletic instructors to prepare students for Gym Drill, and consisted primarily of instruction in the folk dances and the all-school dance that would be performed. In September of 1988, Barbara Chase hired Diana Curran, a professional dancer and choreographer with a degree in dance from Goucher, to further develop the program at Bryn Mawr. The same year, Athletic Director Pat Becker established Dance Company as a varsity sport, with after-school practices and performances throughout the year to "give dancers the credit and recognition that other varsity athletes receive."[21] Dance Company performs at all-school convocations, holiday and end-of-year concerts, and at outside venues including other area schools. Middle School Dance Company meets during the winter season.

Dance instruction in the Lower School is taught in a variety of activities in physical education class, including different folk and square dances supporting the curriculum. The third grade is also prepared for the annual Maypole dance, which opens Bazaar in May. Dance class is required in both Middle and Upper Schools, and prepares the students for Gym Drill dances, but now also incorporates ballet, hip-hop, jazz, modern dance, and tap. There are also dance electives offered in the Upper School.

Piece choreographed by Linda Lloyd-Lee for Dance Company 2010. In the front are Kirsten Adams and Gracie Ogburn

Dance Company members from the Class of 2009 (back to front): Simone Rabinowitz, Catherine Bittar, Stacey Collins, and Ruby Tamborino

Dance Company members from the Class of 2010 (left to right): Leslie Gailloud, Jordan Peters, Isabel van Zijl, Rachel Brown, and Sonya Volsky

Basketball game at Cathedral Street, 1917

Physical education and good health were hallmarks of the school from its inception. The limited quarters available for exercise in the first building that they had rented had restricted the students to exercises and simple games in the courtyard and the basement. The spacious gymnasium in the building at Cathedral Street allowed for the latest exercise and gymnastics equipment, as well as a doctor to serve as athletic director, dedicated to the health and physical improvement of the students. The girls were examined and prescribed daily individual exercise programs by Dr. Kate Hurd, to correct their posture and strengthen specific muscles according to the new methods she had learned from Dr. Dudley Allen Sargent at Harvard, as well as from noted European doctors of the era. The desks and chairs in the silent study room were designed and patented by her successor, Dr. Mary Sherwood, to be adjustable to each student, to ensure correct posture as she studied. Those same desks and chairs were brought to the Study Hall on the Melrose campus and were used by Bryn Mawr girls for many years. During the 1920s, points awarded to the different classes for good posture were posted on a chart, and the competition was recorded in issues of The Quill. In 1950, the posture president, a member of the Athletic Association, was given her own association, which continued to assign demerits and corrective exercises for poor posture. The Posture Association merged in 1960 with the uniform committee of the Student Government Association to become the General Appearance Association.[1] Bryn Mawr students' posture was measured by the school at the beginning of each year into the 1970s.

The continued good health of Bryn Mawr students was remarkable in a city that dealt with frequent epidemics of scarlet fever and rubella, and the school was recognized as an example for the city of Baltimore. Bryn Mawr remained free of the many illnesses that shut down neighboring schools and was only forced to close for a few days during the influenza epidemic in 1918. Fortunately, the girls continued their studies at home, thanks to the dedicated teachers who brought their work to them. In 2010, Bryn Mawr is prepared for uninterrupted academics during pandemic illness through the use of the latest technology. Students and teachers can access assignments electronically and also log in to advanced academic databases for research through the Edith Hamilton Library from home.

"Miss Hamilton's oft quoted reminder to slumping, round-shouldered girls, 'and by her walk the goddess is revealed,' helped at least temporarily to straighten them."

Rosamond Randall Beirne

The Posture Association, we hope, will continue to remind us that chins should be level with the floor, and "wings" flat to the back.

1946 Bryn Mawrtyr

Fencing at Cathedral Street gym, circa 1910

Physical education in the early days included tennis, archery, and fencing, swimming lessons in the school's indoor pool, track and field events, and basketball, with games played between the class teams.[2] Basketball then was an outdoor game played on a court or field, with nine players on each side. In 1901, Edith Hamilton and Miss Carter at St. Timothy's School, then located in Catonsville, agreed to a set of rules for the first game of basketball between the schools. Besides the conduct of players and spectators, it was most important that no girls' names were to be printed in the paper, although *The Sun* did report about the novel game when it was postponed due to weather, and again on November 26, 1901, when Bryn Mawr won 8–7, in front of a crowd of more than 100 spectators. The only male permitted to witness the event was the referee, William Marston, the headmaster of Marston's University School for Boys directly across Cathedral Street from Bryn Mawr, in the building that is now the Maryland State Medical Society. Marston boys were often caught trying to peer over Bryn Mawr's wall while the girls played outside. After this first defeat, the St. Timothy's girls became very serious about beating Bryn Mawr and formed the Brownies and the Spiders, intramural teams that are still active today, to practice more frequently to prepare for the game. They had a decisive advantage, as many of the St. Timothy's girls boarded at the school and could practice more often. After losing to St. Tim's

"I think the greatest excitement that I have ever had in my life was the St. Timothy's Game. Nothing could ever equal the atmosphere that surrounded this one great event of the year. I remember particularly going on a streetcar out to Catonsville where St. Timothy's then was. We were dressed in white flannel blouses with a yellow BMS, and distinguished brown serge bloomers (what a change from our red flannel gym suits). When we acquired this blouse and these bloomers, it was really like receiving a knighthood from the queen. We all had huge yellow chrysanthemums; (St. Timothy's had white chrysanthemums with blue bows)."

Millicent Carey McIntosh, November 4, 1960, in The Bryn Mawr School Bulletin, 1960–1961

for several years, Edith Hamilton divided the Bryn Mawr student body into two teams and a strong intramural competition began that lasted for years. The St. Tim's game, however, continues today as the longest rivalry in girls' scholastic basketball in the country, with only one year's game cancelled due to a measles epidemic.[3]

At Bryn Mawr's 75th anniversary celebration, the distinguished Dr. John E. Bordley confessed that when the school lost to St. Timothy's in 1920 "in attendance were the senior class of the Marston's University School for Boys. They were in fact carefully concealed in hard-coal bin #2 in a nearby coal company, and according to the description of those who survived the contest, it was the dirtiest game they had ever been to."[4]

Basketball team, circa 1915, leaving Montebello for St. Timothy's School

The Garrett property at Montebello, an hour's trolley ride and a half-mile walk from the school, served as makeshift playing fields for the girls, but was used primarily for weekend getaways for groups of students and several teachers. In 1917, the school purchased a vacant lot on Brevard Street, next to the school building on Cathedral, but it was too small for anything other than informal practices. Neither of these properties was truly suited for competitive play.

Basketball continued to be the only game that Bryn Mawr played interscholastically for many years. The game was not moved inside until 1928, when the growing popularity of field hockey as a fall sport shifted basketball to the winter at all the schools in the region.

First field hockey team, 1923

Seniors on the 1964–1965 field hockey team

Several Bryn Mawr girls were members of the English Field Hockey Club, the first women's field hockey team in Baltimore, established at the Baltimore Country Club in October 1911 under the coaching of a Philadelphia woman.[5] When Bryn Mawr began to rent playing fields at Mt. Washington in 1921, Athletic Director Carmen Santos formally introduced her students to field hockey. The sport gained popularity the next year, with larger fields borrowed from the Buckler family and two weeks' work with an excellent English coach, Miss Pearson. According to the 1923 *Bryn Mawrtyr*, "New it was to nearly all, but fascinating, too. It was strenuous exercise; shins were bruised and ankles knocked by an opponent's carelessly mistaking them for the ball."[6] Bryn Mawr's first field hockey game was played against Friends at Mt. Washington on October 26, 1923. Bryn Mawr won that game, 5 to 4, but with "weeping, wailing, and gnashing of teeth" lost to Park School 0 to 7 on October 31, and to Roland Park Country School in a close match, tied to the end, 1 to 2, on November 10.[7] The first student-faculty field hockey game was played the following year.

Field hockey took a strong hold and Bryn Mawr was a frequent host of both inter-city and international games over the years, as well as play-days, which could bring as many as twenty-four public and private schools to its fields.[8]

Constance Applebee, an English physical education teacher, had introduced field hockey to America in 1901 and was hired by M. Carey Thomas as Bryn Mawr College's athletic director in 1904. She was fundamental to field hockey in this country, establishing the United States Field Hockey Association in 1921 and founding the Camp Tegawitha Field Hockey Camp for Girls in Mount Pocono, Pennsylvania in 1923. The camp was held in September or October for three weeks, after the regular summer camp closed for the season. There Carmen Santos met Rosabelle Sinclair, a young British coach who had attempted to introduce the game of girls' lacrosse, developed at her Scottish alma mater, the St. Leonard's School, to students at Rosemary Hall in Connecticut. It didn't take, and when Rosabelle Sinclair accepted The Bryn Mawr School's offer to become the new "Director of Out-Door-Sports," she brought girls' lacrosse to Baltimore. By the spring of 1925, she had the girls throwing lacrosse balls in Bryn Mawr's garden, and *The Quill* noted on March 22, 1925, that "as of yet there are no casualties-and for that let us be thankful–but I am sure that we have nearly all had our share of nervous prostration from dodging wildly waving lacrosse sticks. As soon as warm weather comes all will be well, but now some of the novices seem intent on decapitating their school fellows, or at least Venus de Milo in the front hall."[9] In December of 1925, the fledgling Bryn Mawr School lacrosse team played the first game against three of its own coaches on the newly established All-Baltimore women's team and spent the following spring playing intramural games. In May of 1927, Bryn Mawr played the first interscholastic game against Friends School, winning 13 to 1. The upper field at Bryn Mawr was named for Rosabelle Sinclair in 1978, and in 1993 she was the first woman inducted into the Lacrosse Hall of Fame.

Once the school moved out of the Cathedral Street building to its new expansive twenty-six-acre site, there was ample room for all the students to be involved in athletics every day, rather than the two days a week when Mt. Washington was available to them. By 1930, when the Roland Park Company had prepared the fields, and the locker room was ready, girls as young as the third grade could participate daily in afternoon field hockey, basketball, lacrosse, and tennis, the latter of which had been limited on the previous campus to two courts. To ensure that the smallest girls would be able to learn sports appropriately, two smaller basketball courts were built

Rosabelle Sinclair, 1928

2000 IAAM Championship lacrosse team with Coach Wendy Kridel

Kate Smith, Class of 1998, in action against McDonogh

for them, as was the practice in England. Rosabelle Sinclair eliminated captain's ball, a popular game among the younger students, because it required players to keep one foot in a drawn circle while another player stood on a chair, thus limiting the physicality of the game. An article in the September 28, 1930 *Sun* reiterated Rosabelle Sinclair's belief that "at Bryn Mawr the sport is for the sport's sake, not for the victory it might bring. The playing is the thing, not the ultimate victory or the goals. The aims are skill, enjoyment and benefit, not competition."[10] The students were also involved in much of the management of their sports, and in the 1940s, the Athletic Association chose the varsity team players with assistance from the coaches.

Bryn Mawr girls played volleyball as early as 1921 at Mt. Washington, and they played it frequently as an intramural sport as well as in games against the faculty.[11] Volleyball became a varsity sport in 1989, when forty girls tried out for the new team, led by Dennis Bisgaard, who had played for his native Denmark. Twenty-eight girls were divided into both a varsity and a practice team and played two afternoons a week the first year.[12]

Running has been part of athletics and physical education at Bryn Mawr since the suspended track was included in the 1890 Cathedral Street building. Bryn Mawr held its first track meet at Montebello in 1907, inviting the students from Girls' Latin, Mme. Le Fevre's, Roland Park Country, Arundel, and Lee Schools, where they "ran, jumped, hurled discs and javelins, in spite of the cries of fond mothers and in spite of long corduroy skirts, which tripped them at every step."[13] Track meets were held in the spring for years, until lacrosse became the spring sport in 1926, although races continued to be part of field days in the 1920s and 1930s. In September of 1984, Bryn Mawr cross-country runners joined 160 girls from thirty-two schools in the school's first official meet.[14] The new AIS cross-country conference in 1989 included Bryn Mawr's first varsity team under coaches David Stephens and Barbara Chase.[15] Varsity track was added in 1994 with the use of Gilman's facilities.

Bryn Mawr's 1890 building included two tennis courts in the garden, and two more were available at Montebello; through the early 1920s the school year ended with a tennis tournament, but it was discontinued due to rising interest in other sports. The new campus would provide space for tennis again, and Valerie Penrose, Class of 1932, won the cup at the first revived tournament. The tennis team was soon playing matches against Roland Park Country School. The AIS moved girls' tennis to the fall in September of 1989, as courts at coeducational schools were under increasing demand in the spring. The new fall schedule also provided girls with the opportunity to play after a summer of practice, advancing their level of play.[16]

The Devlin family brought badminton to Bryn Mawr in 1946. Frank J. Devlin, an international champion from Ireland, gave a lecture and presentation to the students, and a club was quickly formed for the four upper classes of the Main School. Members of the varsity team of 1947 won several national tournaments.[17] Susan Devlin, Class of 1949, and her sister, Judy, Class of 1953, would become international champions, winning both singles and pairs titles together. Judy was inducted into the Hall of Fame of USA Badminton in 1963 and that of International Badminton in 1997, and in 1995 was the first inductee into the Hall of Fame of International Women's Sports. In 1976, Susan was also inducted into the US Badminton Hall of Fame, and both sisters were the inaugural inductees into the Hall of Fame of Goucher College in 2010.

Tennis at the Cathedral Street building, circa 1922

Nancy Offutt, Class of 1912

Baseball was one of the first sports played on the concrete pavement of the garden at Cathedral Street and on the fields of Montebello and Mt. Washington. Bryn Mawr girls played baseball or softball off and on over the years as an intramural sport, and in 1976 challenged Gilman to a game and played against Oldfields. On April 12, 1988, the first Bryn Mawr varsity softball team played against Mt. Carmel under Coach Bill Fedock and Athletic Director Pat Becker.[18] The first team practiced on the field below the Gordon Building and hosted games at Gilman, and now has its own home at Mt. Washington.[19]

In 1988–89, Bryn Mawr became the first independent Baltimore girls' school to host a squash team, led by Frank and Nancy Cushman, the women's varsity coaches of Johns Hopkins University. The limited courts available made it difficult to practice for their meets in Pennsylvania, Delaware, and Virginia.[20] Squash continues to travel far afield to compete and challenges a wide variety of teams throughout the Mid-Atlantic region.

Baltimore girls have ridden horses in competitions and hunts for decades, but in the 1990s, Bryn Mawr students competed on a combined St. Timothy's-Bryn Mawr riding team at St. Timothy's facilities.

Winter soccer proved to be a popular addition to athletics, as forty girls tried out in December of 1982. Fall soccer began in September of 1995 at the Herring Run Playday.

The Bryn Mawr crew team began training in 1989 on rowing machines not very different from those imported from England for the school's gymnasium in 1890. The team was soon practicing in two-person shells, quickly moving up to fours and eights, and won their first competition in the spring of 1990.

Bryn Mawr crew team 1999

Three Bryn Mawr students competed as an unofficial team in the Interscholastic Athletic Association of Maryland (IAAM) golf championship in 2003 and won the title over other teams fielding many more players.[21]

Every Bryn Mawr School girl had swimming lessons in the Cathedral Street pool, and seniors in the early 1930s note in their *Bryn Mawrtyr* profiles that they were members of a school swim team from 1928 to 1933. Other than a brief mention of a team competing in 1951 and 1953, there is no other indication of a Bryn Mawr swim team, until the current team was established in 2005–2006.

In 2010, Bryn Mawr's six-year-old ice hockey team wrested the Maryland Scholastic Hockey League championship from Holton-Arms, which had held the title since 2005.

Headmistress Maureen E. Walsh, coach of the 2010 IAAM championship ice hockey team

BRYN MAWR MASCOT

Bryn Mawr and St. Timothy's brought different mascots to the basketball game each year. One year, a younger student dressed in a Bryn Mawr team uniform rode in a cart pulled by a goat; in 1918, a girl was dressed as Uncle Sam. For the fiftieth anniversary game played in 1952, a young student was dressed as a large basketball.[22] For a brief time in the early 1950s, a lamb, named "Daisy" in a contest at the Bazaar, was considered to be the mascot. The first use of "Mawrtian" in a school document seems to be the March 1976 *Quill*, and the Mawrtian call followed soon after, on page 180 of the 1985 *Bryn Mawrtyr*. During the 2006–2007 year, the Athletic Association and Athletic Director Wendy Kridel felt it was time for Bryn Mawr to have an official mascot. Upper School students and faculty voted, and on Spirit Day the official Bryn Mawr mascot was declared to be the Mawrtian.[23]

The Mawrtian Song, 1985 Bryn Mawrtyr

An early Bryn Mawr mascot at the Cathedral Street School Building

GYM DRILL & BANNER MARCH

Margaret Briggs directing Banner March, 1959

"The Grand March" from *Aida*. Teacup. The all-school dance. Stars and bars. Blobs. Passing the banner. These are all vestiges from the earliest days of Bryn Mawr and its dedication to the development of the whole girl, mentally and physically.

Gym Drill is Bryn Mawr's strongest and oldest tradition, passed down from the first classes through five generations of students. It is genuinely unique; a blend of nineteenth-century gymnastics exercises, traditional European folk dances, as well as recently added multicultural and modern dances. Then Banner March, set to "The Grand March" from Verdi's *Aida*, is performed with military precision by hundreds of girls in matching uniforms. It is a celebration of the work of the current students that connects them to the thousands of Bryn Mawr women who came before them. Each Gym Drill requires a year of choreography and careful planning, dance lessons and practices, and its success is dependent on the dedication of the instructors and their students. Girls who were sure they could never learn the Israeli horah, an Italian tarantella, or a Finnish polka, or weave together flat sticks into a star to be held upright while dancing, find themselves on the field doing just those things. Gym Drill unites the school as the students help each other through the steps and brings the community together to celebrate their hard work.

Early indoor gymnasium exhibitions of the 1890s were held so the Bryn Mawr students could demonstrate the physical work they had done over the year, and were a precursor to today's Gym Drill, but as reported in *The Baltimore Sun* involved a variety of activities. At the May 12, 1893, gymnasium exhibition, students swam and dove in the pool, demonstrated Swedish gymnastics, and fenced. They then presented tableaux in full costume, including representations of athletes through time, finishing with scenes of classical Greek athletics.[1] An article from the *Baltimore Evening News*, on April 18, 1896, described another indoor exhibition in which the girls of Bryn Mawr demonstrated the work they had done all year through "muscle and chest exercises, running, jumping, climbing of perpendicular and slanting ropes, as well as vaulting," followed by a game of basketball with teams picked from across the classes. The school cheer was called out so frequently that it was printed in the paper: "Hobble gobble, Hobble gobble, Siss boom bar! Bryn Mawr, Bryn Mawr, 'Rah! 'Rah! 'Rah!'"[2] Students wore gymnasium uniforms of heavy red flannel with matching bloomers, adorned with white cuffs and collars. As the red flannel ran when washed, alumnae reported that the outfits were kept in their lockers at school and dry-cleaned once a year. Black stockings and shoes completed the outfit.[3]

Gym Drill, 1927

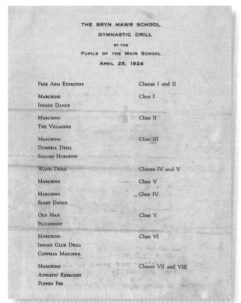
Gymnastic Drill program, 1924

Banner March, 1927

Indian club exercise, 1927

In 1904, Sarah Farquhar, instructor in the gymnasium, finally had perfected the girls' "right about face" and "to the rear–march" to her satisfaction, and began the time-honored tradition of drills and marches. The gymnasium exhibition that year included "wheeling and marching to the rear" and "executing star drills," in addition to the apparatus work. When a group of dignitaries and prominent businessmen from Japan visited Baltimore in November of 1909, *The Sun* noted that their wives were "entertained and greatly interested by a gymnasium drill" held in their honor at Bryn Mawr.[4] By 1911, the exhibition included marching, drilling, and dancing by each class, followed by a grand march by the entire Main School and two dances performed by students selected from each class, and finished with a basketball game.[5]

Seniors Carmen Santos and Anne Murray led the school in the final march in 1913; Miss Santos returned to Bryn Mawr after graduating from the Sargent School of Physical Education in Boston and led the school again in Gym Drill as the instructor. She built upon Mary Elcock's German gymnastics, introduced in 1912, adding more exercises with dumbbells, Indian clubs, and wands. English country dances, a sword dance, and a Russian dance were included for the first time in 1916, and the following year Gym Drill was moved outside to the cement "garden," where for several years the exhibition was accompanied by Louis Fisher's orchestra.[6] After a particularly cold and windy exhibition in March 1919, Edith Hamilton decided to move it back to "the summer days of April or May." Dances that year included a sailor's hornpipe, a Polish mazurka, and an Irish jig, although the classes waited inside for their turns and had to rely on their parents' assurance that their class would certainly win the gymnasium cup that year at graduation.[7] By 1922, the red flannel suit was changed to a blue suit with white blouse, and was soon changed from that to a more form-fitting brown tunic.[8]

Gym Drill, 1960s

In the mid-1920s, Rosabelle Sinclair reduced the complicated marches and drills and introduced traditional British folk dances and exercises that improved balance and coordination. She was a formidable instructor and used her distinctly sharp British voice to command a student to stop slumping or take a step to the left, often from across a field surrounded by parents. She deeply believed that every girl could improve and excel, and she constantly urged her students to do so. She rewarded their hard work with gym "bars" for their performance in gymnastics and dance classes, and a star for those who had previously earned two bars, calling them in front of the entire school to be recognized at Gym Drill.[9] The badges were sewn onto the students' gym tunics, which were often worn throughout the school day. Seniors who had received

Norma Simmons assists with vaulting at Gym Drill, 1960s

a bar each year were awarded a silver cup at their final Gym Drill. Margaret Briggs, Class of 1930 and later Miss Sinclair's assistant and successor, would recall in a *Quill* interview in February 1975, that while other institutions may have had some kind of a gym drill, none were like Bryn Mawr's, which was "really an English one . . . that gets personally passed on. Miss Sinclair passed it to me, and I passed it to Miss Simmons."[10]

Blair Stambaugh presents an award at Gym Drill, 1980

Over the years there was greater variation in the drills and dances chosen. In 1956, folk dances from England, Norway, Russia, and Sweden were included, and two years later acrobatics, from Main I somersaults to Upper School vaulting were added. In 1971, dances from Israel and Greece were added, while in more recent years Diana Curran has introduced dances from all over the world, reflecting Bryn Mawr's greater diversity and global perspective. The senior dance in the 1930s and 1940s was often a Russian or Swedish folk dance in full costume, while the class of 1965 dressed as Italian peasants to perform a tarantella.[11] In 1968, a new green, pleated tunic with a sash that tied on the side replaced the straight brown tunic with a buttoned belt.[12]

The Gym Drill of 1985 brought every Bryn Mawr student to the field, nearly eight hundred in all, with older students partnered with the younger ones in the all-school dance. Every class from 1915–1984 was represented in the 500-strong Alumnae Banner March, and some 300 followed Norma Simmons in an alumnae dance.

Louise Allen Armstrong, Class of 1938, marching with the daughters of Carrie Armstrong Montague, Class of 1980; Jessie 2016, Eliza 2012, and Isabel 2013.

"Every Bryn Mawr graduate has indelible memories of Gym Drill, including whitening sneakers, marching in formation, standing on a white 'blob' painted on the field, dancing with ankle bells, swords, or scarves."

Suzanne Feldman Rosenthal, Class of 1972, Communiqué, 2004

Running for awards

Gym Drill in jumpers and colored sashes

"Let it Whip," a very modern and energetic all-school dance in 1989, generated conversation about tradition and change at Bryn Mawr. For those students who did not particularly enjoy learning and performing century-old exercises and dances for the sake of tradition, the inclusion of such a contemporary piece made them question the historic value of Gym Drill. "It should either be Gym Drill like it used to be or not at all," summed up one sophomore in the May 4, 1990 *Quill*.[13] For others, it exemplified how traditions can be adapted to reflect current times and remain relevant without losing their connection to the past.[14] Over the years, many Bryn Mawr alumnae have found that Gym Drill, no matter how they felt about it as a student, has become one of their most poignant memories, and they enjoy returning to join the Banner March in their reunion years.

In 1990, in celebration of Barbara Chase's ten years as headmistress, each class presented her with a plate the students had painted to represent their dance or the country from which it came. The following year brought a special addition to Gym Drill dances, as the Middle School Black Awareness Club performed an African dance.[15]

Traditional Morris sword dance performed by 9th graders. Ellie McLaughlin, Erica Matz, Julia Clemens, Myra Hyder (holding star), Laney Mann, Molly Wolf, and Anna Feiss, members of the Class of 2012

"It was pretty stressful being school captain with having to remember all of the dance steps and trying not to fumble too badly through my speech; standing at the podium, however, presented a pretty awesome sight— hundreds of young women enjoying the weather, their peers, and the spirit of tradition, some without even realizing it."

Jennifer J. Ahn, Class of 2000

The Gym Drill of 1995 was the last in which the entire Middle and Upper Schools wore the green gym tunic, which continues to be worn now only for the ninth-grade sword dance.[16] A new white and yellow sash was designed, embroidered with the daisy and the student's class year. Each year the students sew on the back of the sash a ribbon of that grade's color, originally assigned in the late 1920s by Rosabelle Sinclair. Stars and bars are applied to the front, as are commemorative badges such as those designed for the Centennial Gym Drill, celebrated in 2004, and for the school's 125th anniversary, in 2010.

For more than a year, Bryn Mawr athletics instructor and coach Jeanette Budzik guided a team of thirty Upper School students to research and conduct interviews with alumnae about their memories of Gym Drill. The video they produced for the Centennial Gym Drill provides insight into the important role that this time-honored tradition holds for alumnae, and it captures the bond that Gym Drill has created for the entire Bryn Mawr community.

There is no indication when class banners were included in the grand march that ended early Gym Drills, but Mary Gould Ellicott, Class of 1916, remembered that "the banner wasn't given to one person. We took turns. It was very important to carry the banner; it was a great honor."[17] For decades, each Gym Drill has ended with the Banner March, in which the class captains, chosen by the dance instructors and the class, pass their banner down to the class behind them and accept the banner of the class they will become. The fifth grade marches onto the field for the first time to join the Middle School, leaving behind them the Lower School. Seniors are left without a banner, in anticipation of their graduation as new Bryn Mawr alumnae. Instead, the junior class showers the seniors with daisies as they leave the field.

Amy Daniels, Julia Hemmendinger, Lacey Hankin, and Bailey Johnson, Class of 2010

For many years, Gym Drill music was performed by Margery Wagner (back) on drums and Evelyn Stone on piano, 1976

Class dances, Gym Drill, 2010

BAZAAR & MAYPOLE

Bryn Mawr Bazaar, 1961

Bryn Mawr's first spring Bazaar was held by the Parents Association on May 5, 1948 to support the building fund of the school. There had been many small fund-raising efforts by parents and alumnae since the school had moved to the Melrose campus, and Katharine Van Bibber suggested they instead organize into one "great cooperative effort."[1] During World War I, students and parents sold baked goods and crafts at small bazaars to support Belgian Relief and the Red Cross. To raise money to purchase the new campus and to pay off the loans in the 1920s and 1930s, parents and alumnae sponsored lectures and ticket sales for opera productions, and held pony shows, dances, and card parties, as well as bazaars, raising several hundred dollars at a time.[2]

Lower School has opened Bazaar for years with a Maypole Dance, by the kindergarten in the 1960s, the second grade from 1970-1995, and by the third grade since 1996. The earliest documented Maypole at Bryn Mawr was on Alumnae Day on May 1, 1936. Bryn Mawr girls also have danced the Maypole at Flowermart as early as 1983.

Although it was held on a cold and rainy day, the first Bazaar raised more money than anticipated, and parents asked to hold another the following year so that they could continue to work together for the school's benefit. From the Alumnae Association's flower booth, games, pony rides, and items for sale, including Katharine Van Bibber's homemade cookies, to fathers of the senior class in chef's hats carving at sit-down suppers, and a toy symphony that delighted the children, Bazaar brought everyone together to enjoy the day while they worked to support the school.[3]

From 1948 to 1978, Bazaar was held after morning classes on the first Wednesday of May, while Gym Drill was held on the following Wednesday afternoon. For several years, Bazaars went late into the evening, with sit-down dinners and faculty shows, ending as late as ten o'clock. In 1958, the full dinners were replaced with more mobile fare, and the faculty show was moved to another evening, coinciding with a class play or Dramatic Club presentation, which permitted an earlier closing. In 1979, Bazaar was moved to Friday morning, and since 1987, it has been held on Saturday. Bazaar has truly been an all-school event, with each class responsible for organizing games, activities, and events; parents organizing the used book sale, cooking and selling food, and donating items for sale; and the alumnae sponsoring their flower booth. Bazaar would not be possible without the dedication of the staff and faculty, who work for weeks to prepare and host the event.

Lemonsticks are a perennial favorite at Bryn Mawr's Bazaar.

GRADUATION

Nancy Bucher, far right, leads the Class of 1931 into the Graduation Garden

On June 9, 1893, the first graduation ceremony was held to recognize the ten girls, past and present, who had successfully completed the school program and passed the college entrance exams. There were two "graduates" each from the Classes of 1888, 1890, and 1892, who had already either graduated from or were enrolled in Bryn Mawr College, as well as four girls from the Class of 1893. They were regaled by Paul du Chaillu's stories of his adventures in equatorial Africa, where he was the

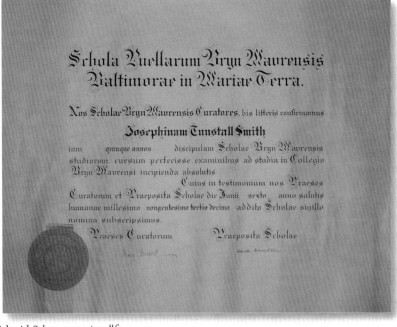

first Westerner to discover gorillas and certain pygmy tribes.[1] Later speakers would include Julia Ward Howe in 1898, Henry James in 1905, and former President William Howard Taft in 1915, as M. Carey Thomas would arrange for them to speak at the graduations of both Bryn Mawrs, and accompany them on the train from the college to the school.

The first diplomas were awarded the next year, on June 9, 1894, and were written in Latin. They bore "a seal device of daisies, the flower of Bryn Mawr School and College. . . which comprises the colors of the institutions, yellow and white."[2] The word "daisy" comes from the Old English *dæges eage*, or "day's eye," as the flower's petals open with the dawn and close at sunset.[3] In the school seal, the sun is represented by a young woman, with the flower's petals drawing upward to her. The school motto, *Ex Solo Ad Solem*, meaning "from the earth to the sun," encircles the image and completes the symbolism of "the relationship of the daisy to the sun—and metaphorically, of the child's mind to truth and wisdom."[4] This was the first appearance of the school seal, as an impression in a thick yellow wax circle, that was pinned to the diploma along with yellow and white ribbon. The heavy and fragile wax seal was replaced in 1934 with a paper seal.

Early graduation ceremonies were held in the school's gymnasium, on a temporary stage decorated with daisy chains and palm trees. Graduating girls wore white frocks, with yellow ribbons in their hair and sometimes a yellow sash, and they carried white baskets that were filled with daisies by their younger school friends. As the number of students, graduates, and families grew, the ceremony moved outdoors to the garden, or to a local church in the event of rain.

Class advisor Steve Amann looks on as Gabby Bittrick, Class of 2008, receives her diploma from President of the Board of Trustees Georgia D. Smith, Class of 1972

The terraced garden behind Gordon has been the setting for graduation since the acquisition of the Melrose campus, but in the first few years the graduates walked up onto the porch to shake hands with the president of the board of managers, while the audience sat in the garden facing the porch. Rain has been a consistent threat to the beautiful Graduation Garden setting, but locusts have remained a seventeen year challenge, leading Diane Howell in 1970 to leave a letter of warning for the headmistress of June 1987: "we had been warned by the survivors of what was known as Commencement in 1953 who had been outdoors, that the situation was impossible; locusts crawled up legs, flew down dress necks, and made such a din that the speakers could not be heard. But the unbelievers and the young refused to believe that the situation could be so bad as to force us indoors. Days, weeks went by, and it seemed possible to plan on an outdoor ceremony. Finally, just a few days before graduation, the creatures emerged in earnest and set up their song. It was all true. It would have been impossible in the garden."[5]

Strong rain showers have plagued late afternoon graduation ceremonies in recent years, but seniors have been reluctant to give up the procession from the porch of Gordon into the Graduation Garden. In 2009, determined that the students would have their procession, Maureen Walsh conducted the ceremony as planned. The girls proceeded to their places on stage, and then the entire community picked up and moved indoors to finish the ceremony in Centennial Hall, as the rains came down. Graduation now takes place earlier in the day to avoid these common later afternoon rains.

> "When we finally trundled our daisy baskets up the steps of the Congregational Church (because it rained on graduation day) we had a genuine sense of accomplishment and a subtle feeling that, through the fires of discipline, we had somehow been tempered to adulthood."
>
> *Anne Kinsolving Brown, Class of 1924*
> *Alumnae of the Year address, May 20, 1964*

Marielana Kirwin, Kathilynch Smith, Corrine Coppola, Nina Colhoun, Tamala Rice, and Stephanie Brosso, Class of 1984

Far Right: Lisa Curlett, Nikki Gilliam, Jennifer DeLuca, Karin Walser, Mary Ellen Chandler, and Lisa Lebow, Class of 1984

Dr. Jane McAuliffe, President, Bryn Mawr College, 2010

Dr. Julia Haller Gottsch, Class of 1972, speaks on a rainy graduation day in 2009

Whitney Ransome, Director of the National Coalition for Girls Schools, 2006

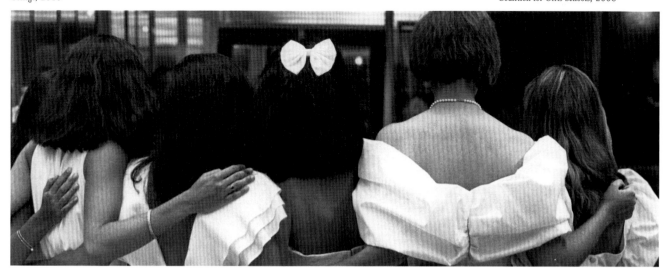

EDITH HAMILTON

"Civilization is a matter of
delight in things of the mind."

The Greek Way

Edith Hamilton at Seawall, Mount Desert Isle, Maine, where she did much of her writing

Edith Hamilton's second career as a prolific and successful author began shortly after her retirement from Bryn Mawr. Her close friends in New York at *Theatre Arts Monthly* were enthralled with her lively and fascinating explanations of the literature of the Greek and Roman classical world. Her passion and comprehension of the ancient world, combined with an innate talent for storytelling that Bryn Mawr students adored, brought to life the oldest tales of modern civilization for them. Her friends urged her to share the ancient world with a wider audience, and at the age of sixty Edith Hamilton began to publish articles and wrote a translation of Aeschylus' *Prometheus*. In 1930, her first book, *The Greek Way*, was published to wide acclaim and later revised and reissued as *The Great Age of Greek Literature*. It was followed in 1932 by *The Roman Way* and in 1936 by *Prophets of Israel*. Among her many other publications were *Three Greek Plays: Prometheus Bound, Agamemnon, The Trojan Women; Witness to the Truth; Mythology; Spokesmen for God; The Echo of Greece;* and *The Ever-Present Past*, as well as numerous articles and book reviews in *The New York Times Book Review* and *The Saturday Review*.

A White House invitation, 1962

Although she never finished her doctoral studies in Europe, Edith Hamilton was awarded several honorary doctorates in her later years from Goucher College, the University of Pennsylvania, the University of Rochester, and Yale University. Among her many honors, she received the Jane Addams Medal for Distinguished Service from Rockford College and the Constance Lindsay Skinner Award of the Women's National Book Association; she was elected to the American Academy of Arts and Letters, and she was honored by the Women's National Press Club. She declined the invitation as a "Great Thinker" to John F. Kennedy's inauguration. Robert Kennedy quoted her writing when speaking of the death of his brother and of Dr. Martin Luther King Jr., and many believe that it was First Lady Jacqueline Kennedy who gave her brother-in-law Edith Hamilton's writings to ease his mourning.

Receiving her honorary doctorate at Yale University, June 9, 1959. Front: Ellsworth Bunker, United States ambassador to India; Potter Stewart, associate justice of the United States Supreme Court; A. Whitney Griswold, president of Yale University; Edith Hamilton, author and educator; Gunnar Myrdal, Swedish economist and diplomat; James Lee Loomis, Yale University. Rear: Elia Kazan, director; Ernst Mayr, evolutionary biologist, Harvard University; Rev. David H. C. Head, pastor, New Haven; William E. Hocking, philosopher, Harvard University; Murray Gell-Mann, physicist, California Institute of Technology; Duncan Phillips, director of the Phillips Gallery, Washington, D.C.

Of all the honors that Edith Hamilton received, she was most proud of those awarded to her just before her 90th birthday, on August 8, 1957. Standing on the stage of the theatre of Herodes Atticus at the foot of the Acropolis after a bilingual presentation of her translation of *Prometheus Bound*, the mayor of Athens bestowed Athenian citizenship upon her, in recognition of all she had done to honor Greek civilization over the years. Earlier that day, King Paul of Greece had presented her with the nation's highest honor, the Golden Cross of the Order of Benefaction.[1]

Edith Hamilton died on May 31, 1963, at the age of 95, while she was still at work on another book about Plato. Her close friend, the noted writer John Mason Brown, wrote of her in *The Saturday Review* just after her death: "Nobility of mind, character, and spirit is rare indeed. Wisdom, true wisdom, is no less rare. Edith, one of the most human of mortals, was the radiant possessor of both, as is made clear on one exalting page after another."[2] Edith Hamilton's wisdom and her personal quest for knowledge and understanding were well instilled at Bryn Mawr, and continue to guide the school today.

"At all times those people are few and far between who can indeed, who must–be described as having nobility of mind and spirit. It is to this slim fellowship that Miss Hamilton belongs."

John Mason Brown

Edith Hamilton receiving her honors in Athens, Greece, 1957

TRADITIONS

Bryn Mawr was founded as a nonsectarian school, but the Christian beliefs of the founders and early school community were reflected in the values and traditions of the school. Each day began with the students gathered in the Study Hall, where Edith Hamilton or Clara Crane would read a Bible passage, and everyone would recite the "Lord's Prayer" together. The day's schedule would be announced, and the students would go to class. In 1908, Edith Hamilton adapted "For a Birthday" from the *Book of Common Prayer* to suit the school's purpose, and the resulting Bryn Mawr School Prayer was repeated daily by generations of Bryn Mawr girls.[1] Communal singing of a hymn was added soon thereafter, leading to greater interest in music in school, the hiring of a music teacher, and the establishment of the first glee club in 1923.

Edith Hamilton loved to read the passage from "Philippians 4.8," "Whatsoever things are true…" which Katharine Van Bibber also read frequently as headmistress, as well as verses on charity from "1 Corinthians." These Christian prayers and New Testament readings were meant to remind the students to consider their actions and thoughts, to be mindful of their community and the world around them, and to live purposeful lives. Helen M. Bowdoin, Class of 1956, noted that "We realized the concepts of sharing and giving, of selflessness and forgiveness, of charity were recurring themes that [Katharine Van Bibber] wanted to instill."[2] In 1985, Barbara Landis Chase, after consulting with ecumenical leaders, proposed to change the word "cross" to "light" in the school prayer to embrace and reflect the more varied religious backgrounds of the school community.

SCHOOL PRAYER

Watch over our school, O Lord, as its years increase, and bless and guide its children wherever they may be, keeping them ever unspotted from the world.

Let their hearts be pure, their faith unshaken, their principles immovable.

Be thou by their side if dark hours shall come upon them; strengthen them when they stand; comfort and help them when they are weakhearted; raise them up if they fall.

Let thy light never grow dim to their eyes, but through the struggle and the business of their everyday lives, let its radiance lead them heavenward, and in their hearts may thy peace which passeth understanding abide all the days of their lives.

Prayers in the Elizabeth Thomas Auditorium, 1967

A Christmas pageant, 1964

Four juniors established the Christian Association in 1940, to bring clerics of different denominations to the school to talk about religion and ethics. The association soon began to organize a program for Bryn Mawr students to volunteer at Union Memorial Hospital and was responsible for prayers once a week. In 1955, silent prayer was introduced, and more variety was brought to prayers by having different classes organize the meetings. On November 28, 1955, Tina Patterson of the Class of 1956 conducted an entire prayer program in French, for which the students practiced translated prayers and hymns. By 1960, there were 150 girls in Christian Association meeting once a week to hear speakers and plan a variety of volunteer projects, from working with needy children to helping at local hospitals and nursing homes. Christian Association also raised funds for charitable institutions. Interest in religious topics gave way in the latter half of the 1960s to issues of social change, political matters, and a greater desire to hear and talk about subjects of more immediate concern, such as poverty, crime, drugs and alcohol, and women's issues. Christian Association and Speaker's Club merged in 1970 under the leadership of Blair Barton and Margaret Perry, Class of 1971, as the organizations shared similar missions of providing presentations on timely topics. The new organization was named Symposium, and Morning Prayers became Morning Convocation.[3] Convocation has continued to provide a time for the school to come together for presentations by students, clubs, and faculty as well as outside speakers.

In 1904, the class of 1906 decided to present a Christmas play for the school, beginning a tradition for the ninth grade that lasted through the 1930s. The Primary School had, by then, developed its own Christmas Pageant based on tableaux of master artwork depicting Christmas themes. The young students dressed in costume and posed in position to represent the different paintings or sculptures, and then sang traditional Christmas carols. By 1940, the Glee Clubs and Dramatic Club became part of a similar Main School pageant, replacing the play, with the Art Department preparing the staging. In the 1950s, members of the Dramatic Club began to add Bible recitations, and Stage Club took over the sets. The pageant became so popular that first two, and then three, performances had to be presented by different groups of students in each. Construction of the Elizabeth Thomas Auditorium provided enough space so that everyone could be involved again in one large performance. The student body sang, and handbells and other instruments were included. Rather than presenting a series of different tableaux as in the past, students costumed as members of the Nativity would gather together on a platform until the entire scene was displayed. The pageant traditionally began with "Masters in This Hall" and ended with "On This Day." During the week leading up to the pageant, Bible passages were recited during prayers. As the school community became more diverse, the musical aspects of the pageant became the center of the seasonal celebrations, and by the end of the 1980s, Winterlore, "a seasonal celebration of song, dance, and drama depicting winter's promise of renewal" was presented along with holiday concerts.[4] Today, Bryn Mawr celebrates the holidays and significant events of several different religions and cultures of the school community, both in the classroom and through performance.

Winterlore, 1993

Another holiday tradition begun in the winter of 1904 by the Class of 1906 was to prepare boxes of food, clothing, and gifts for needy families in the city. Boxpacking has been a time-honored tradition ever since, as Bryn Mawr girls and faculty have contributed to and prepared much-appreciated packages as part of the holiday season.

Boxpacking, 1981

School songs

Bryn Mawr has two official school songs. In 1908, Mary Tongue of the Class of 1909 wrote a song for the entire school, set to the music of Ethelbert Nevin's "Canzona Amorosa." For many years, the school sang this song at major events.

"Joyous the Love" is sung more commonly today by the entire school. Written by members of the Class of 1936, it is set to the music of a Welsh air.

A BRYN MAWR SCHOOL SONG

Joyous the love

That rises in our heart;

To thee, Bryn Mawr, we sing

Of thy dear world apart;

Thy happy halls, thy fearless world

Of calm and strife, where hope unfurled

Wild dreams of youth, a wakening world

Of wider realms a part.

Shout, shout the love

Our praise to thee, Bryn Mawr

For golden hopes and dreams

That shine where 'er we are

In sorrow, joy, in wisdom's quest

In work, in play, achievement's zest,

If years from now we meet the test,

We'll thank thee then, Bryn Mawr!

Middle School music teacher Sherrell Dameron leads the choir at Commencement as Music Department Chair Jan Bishop accompanies on the piano

Choral practice, 1960s

Bryn Mawrtyr, 1909

JERUSALEM

And did those feet in ancient time

Walk upon England's mountain green?

And was the Holy Lamb of God

On England's pleasant pastures seen?

And did the countenance divine

Shine forth upon our clouded hills?

And was Jerusalem builded here

Among these dark satanic mills?

Bring me my bow of burning gold!

Bring me my arrows of desire!

Bring me my spear! O clouds, Unfold!

Bring me my chariot of fire!

I will not cease from mental fight,

Nor shall my sword sleep in my hand,

Til we have built Jerusalem

In England's green and pleasant land.

Preparing for a concert, 1960s

The song "Jerusalem," sung today by Day-seye at all-school convocations, concerts, and graduation, has been part of Bryn Mawr's traditions for decades. "Jerusalem" serves both Bryn Mawr and England as an unofficial anthem, chosen in 2010 by popular vote to be played for the English teams at the Commonwealth Games, and used by national cricket and rugby teams, as well as the women's lacrosse team when they compete. The song was created in 1916, at the suggestion of the British poet laureate Robert Bridges, who asked Sir Hubert Parry to set to music the words of William Blake's 1804 preface to his poem on Milton to encourage the English at a time of low morale during World War I. Sir Hubert conducted "Jerusalem" himself at a March 1918 celebratory meeting for the British suffragette movement, as he was friends with two of the most noted members, Agnes Garrett and Millicent Fawcett. The song quickly became an anthem for the women's movement.[5] The first documentation of "Jerusalem" at Bryn Mawr comes from Amy Kelly, writing of leaving the Cathedral Street building in the 1931 *Bryn Mawrtyr*: "And with us, too, will go the storied image of the old

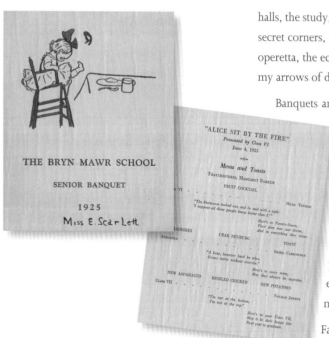

THE BRYN MAWR SCHOOL

SENIOR BANQUET

1925

Miss E. Scarlett

"ALICE SIT BY THE FIRE"
Presented by Class VI
June 4, 1925

Menu and Toasts
TOASTMISTRESS, MARGARET BARKER

FRUIT COCKTAIL

halls, the study, the library, the memory of conferences on the stairs, confidences in secret corners, winter fires, the scent of Christmas greens, the glamour of play and operetta, the echo of 'Ideo-O-O,' of 'Bring me my bow of burning gold, Bring me my arrows of desire,' of the shout for the trophy and the hanging of the banner."

Banquets and plays were a favorite way for one class to honor another. Sister classes would host one another during the school year by putting on a play and hosting a banquet, but the most important event for many years was the Junior-Senior Banquet. The junior class chose a theme, decorated the gym, wrote invitations and menus, and made up songs or toasts about different aspects of the senior class and the year nearly completed. The sophomores put on a play to entertain everyone, and then were permitted to sit on the suspended running track above to watch the banquet. The play was eventually eliminated, and seniors continued to enjoy a banquet for many years as part of the graduation festivities.

Father-daughter dinners were popular all-school events, beginning in 1949 and running through the early 1960s. Father-daughter picnics and other events were held on a smaller scale into the 1990s.

Balloon ascensions were used as celebratory and fund-raising endeavors for more than thirty years at Bryn Mawr. In the 1950s, balloons were sold at Bazaar with a ticket bearing instructions for the finder to mail it back to the school, and the person whose balloon traveled the farthest would win a prize. Balloon tickets were mailed back from Chincoteague, the Eastern Shore, and Delaware; one balloon was found bobbing in the ocean and brought back by a fishing party. Through the 1970s and mid-1980s, SGA sponsored balloon ascensions to raise funds for the United Way, and Lower Schoolers launched balloons on November 6, 1981, as part of the tenth anniversary celebrations for their buildings.

The first Founders Day celebration kicked off the centennial year on September 21, 1984, with commemorations by Mayor Schaefer, Senator Sarbanes, and Lt. Governor Curran to honor the school. In 1987, faculty awards were first presented on Founders Day, rather than at Commencement. Teachers portrayed the founders and early faculty, in a play written by Middle School English and drama teacher Michael Robinson in 2000, and the school celebrated the new bridges connecting the tricoordinate schools in 2001.

Upper School faculty members as Bryn Mawr's founders: Arna Margolis as Julia Rogers, Mary Armstrong Shoemaker (standing), Class of 1969, as Mamie Gwinn, and Jackie Sanders as M. Carey Thomas, Founders Day, 2000.

There has been a class ring at Bryn Mawr since at least 1909, but for decades each class chose its own design. Bailey Banks & Biddle, Philadelphia, advertised in the 1933 *Bryn Mawrtyr* that they were the "Designers and Makers of the Official Bryn Mawr School 1933 Class Ring."[6] In 1963, Diane Howell suggested that the Class of 1965 institute a school design. According to *The Quill*, in March of 1963, the ring would "be gold of medium size with an oval school seal raised on the top. Several classes which have now graduated have had this ring as their class ring."[7] In more recent years, Bryn Mawr students also have had the option of a stone with the seal engraved. The sophomore class celebrates receiving the school ring with the Ring Dance, held in the Dance Studio.

Seniors choose an underclassman to help them ring the bell in the Class of 1992 Belltower, before leaving campus to pursue their senior projects. The belltower, which provides elevator access to the three levels of Howell, was funded by the Senior Parent Gift of 1992.

Class Day began as practice for the graduation exercises. Awards are presented to students, and gavels are passed to the next leaders of student associations.

Anna, Class of 2012, and Julia, Class of 2017, help their cousin Maggie Feiss, Class of 2004, ring the bell.

Class rings of Barbara Johnson Bonnell, Class of 1948, and Sandra Di Cataldo, Class of 2012

Associate Headmistress Peggy Bessent presenting awards on Class Day, 2007

Cynthia Murray and kindergarten students admiring their gingerbread houses

LOWER SCHOOL TRADITIONS

The Lower School at Bryn Mawr has its own unique set of traditions that bring young girls together through a variety of fun, educational projects. As new girls join the classes each year, the "older" girls quickly teach them the words to the Bryn Mawr prayer and *Joyous the Love*, how and where to line up for class, where to store the bin for their belongings, as well as their favorite playground games. Each class also undertakes several traditional projects every year.

First graders learn about different animals as they anxiously wait for duck eggs to hatch and then help care for the ducklings, as well as taking the traditional trip to the farm of former Bryn Mawr teacher Mrs. Cynthia Murray.

As second grade students study the pioneer movement, they learn nineteenth-century crafts and plan their own trips across the country in a Conestoga wagon. Their studies end with the Pioneer Picnic, which they enjoy with their parents.

The imaginary trip to France has been a highlight of third-grade French classes for decades. Students pack their luggage, plan their trip, and send back postcards and letters to their families.

Members of the Class of 1988 ready to depart on their imaginary trip to France with teacher Betsy Tomlinson

Raina Coleman, Class of 2015, with her mother, at the International Bazaar, 2007

Fifth grader Catherine Bittar, Class of 2009, at the annual Newbery Award Luncheon in 2002. Begun in 1974, fifth-grade students read nominated books and select their own winner for the presitgious award. A noted author attends the luncheon to talk with the girls about the art of writing and to view the students' own literary projects.

The fourth grade held its first International Bazaar in the Old Gym on April 30, 1971, after formulating the plan themselves in February while working on their country reports. Students from across the school enjoyed "Cuban coconut, Irish bread, French fudge, Greek baklava, German cookies, and Australian dip" also known as pavlova.[8]

In the spring, the fifth-grade students relinquish their morning car door opening duties for five days at Echo Hill. They sleep in open cabins, explore and learn about the Chesapeake Bay and the environment, and come together as a class before heading "up the hill" to Middle School.

Erica Boyd, Tina Pappas, Avendui Shoup, Kelly Rogers, Eva Vishio, Candy Calon, Rori Bloom, and Bari Rudikoff, Class of 1989, at Echo Hill, 1982

FACULTY

A wise teacher has said that a sense for quality is the final test of the educated person.
This sense, sure and uncompromising, is not given us by fiat.
It grows from the quiet experiences in class-rooms where we come at the substance of
learning in company with those scholar-teachers, themselves lovers of learning,
who have been the essential glory of Bryn Mawr.

Amy Kelly, 1931 Bryn Mawrtyr

Please refer to page 211 for captions for the following photographs

Faculty of The Bryn Mawr School, 1923

Celebrating 125 YEARS

Trustee Nancy Ratcliffe Ferrell, Class of 1975, led a team of dedicated and hard-working volunteers as chair of the 125th anniversary celebrations held throughout the year. On opening day, the campus was decorated with festive balloon sculptures and banners bearing the anniversary logo. The faculty, staff, and students from Little School to the senior class gathered on the Rosabelle Sinclair Field to cheer as an airplane overhead snapped a commemorative photograph on September 21, the first day of school in 1885. (1) Art projects throughout the divisions explored the school's founding and history. Among the many projects created, Middle School student Hadley Brown, Class of 2015, drew a Victorian Bryn Mawr portrait, (2) while Little School students made owls (3) and a paper version of the school mosaic (4). In the spring, Professor Elliott Shore brought faculty and students from his class on the history of Bryn Mawr College to campus as part of a tour of the Baltimore roots of the two institutions.

(5) Author Kathleen Waters Sander, left, with Bryn Mawr parents Pat Meisol and Gary Goldberg, spoke about the life of founder Mary Elizabeth Garrett during Middle and Upper School convocations and on Alumnae Weekend. Bryn Mawr celebrated with a spectacular party in the Graduation Garden that evening. The Gordon Drive was lined with students greeting alumnae with reunion class banners (6).

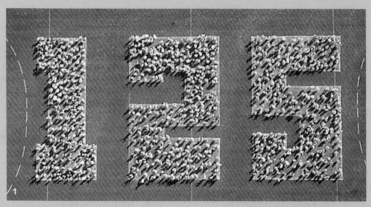

Deb Ross Chambliss, Class of 1970, Ethel Wagandt Galvin and Katherine Teensa Ryland Williams, both Class of 1945, reminisced while viewing the photographic timeline that was on display throughout the campus during the anniversary year (7). Julie Smith Marshall, Class of 1989 and Jennie Lee Williams Fowlkes, Class of 1965 (8), and Christine and Stephen Rogers with Susan Reid Mills (9) enjoyed the party outside.

Inside, alumnae identified copies of photographs for the archives (10) and shared stories over a yearbook. (11) Suzanne Feldman Rosenthal, Class of 1972, and Mary Hundley DeKuyper, Class of 1956 (12) enjoyed the events of the evening.

Ann Hankin, Maureen Walsh, and Nancy Ferrell cut the 125th anniversary cake (13) during the party. The next day, Gym Drill and Banner March were performed in front of a large anniversary banner that had been displayed in Baltimore during the year (14). In the fall of 2010, Headmistress Maureen Walsh spoke about single-sex education for girls at Bryn Mawr College's anniversary conference, which brought participants from colleges, universities, and girls' schools from around the world. Former Bryn Mawr headmistresses Blair Stambaugh, Katy Dallam, and Barbara Landis Chase returned to campus on Founders Day to conclude the anniversary celebrations. Barbara Landis Chase, Head of School at Phillips Academy, Andover, since leaving Bryn Mawr in 1994, spoke to the school community (15).

1885-2010

TIMELINE

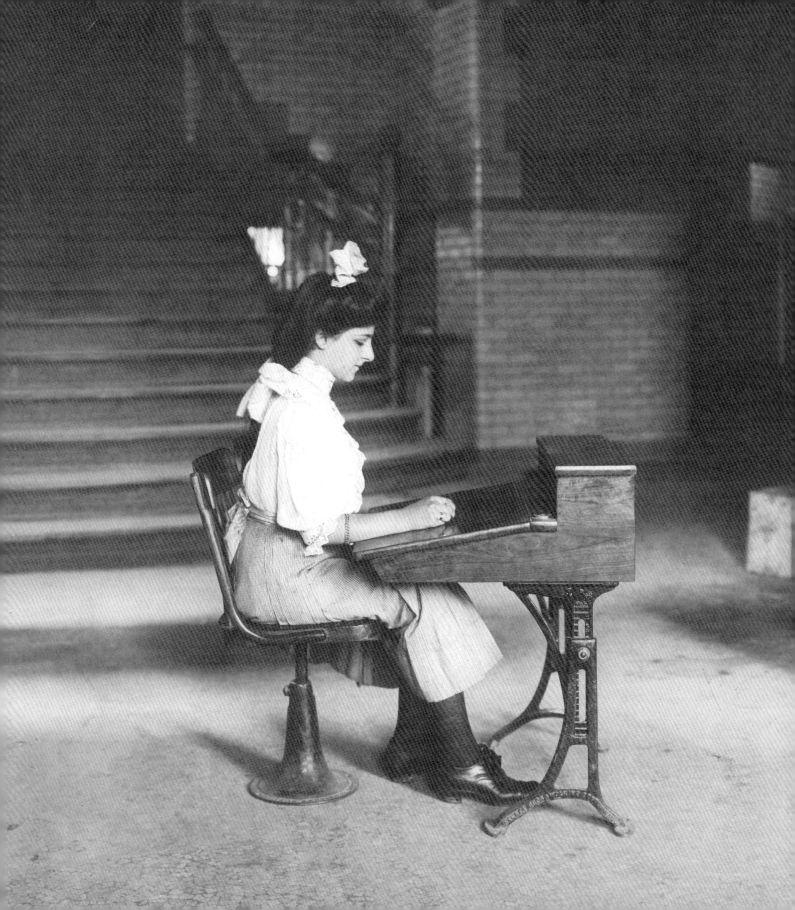

FOUNDING A SCHOOL

1800s

1885

M. Carey Thomas, Mary Elizabeth Garrett, Mary Mackall Gwinn, Elizabeth Tabor King, and Julia Rebecca Rogers found The Bryn Mawr School to provide girls with a college-preparatory education, which includes studies in French, German, Greek, history, Latin, and mathematics.

The first session opens in a rented building behind the Quaker Meeting House on Eutaw Street, with a handful of students and eight teachers.

1890

Mary Elizabeth Garrett finances the construction of a unique school building on the corner of Cathedral and Preston Streets, the present-day site of the Meyerhoff Symphony Hall. The building includes a science laboratory, a library, an art studio with skylights, and classrooms filled with classical art and sculpture. The state-of-the-art gymnasium has a suspended running track, indoor swimming pool, and "needle baths," known today as showers.

1893

The first school diplomas are presented. The diplomas are decorated with the new school seal, which features a sunburst, an open flower, and the school motto, "Ex Solo Ad Solem," from the earth to the sun. A formal Alumnae Association begins to take shape.

Mary Elizabeth Garrett, encircled by, from lower left, M. Carey Thomas, Mamie Gwinn, Bessie King, and Julia Rogers

1894

The founders establish a Primary to teach six- and seven-year-old girls how to read, write, and "work in numbers." The curriculum includes French, science, drawing, and gymnastics.

1896

Edith Hamilton, a distinguished Bryn Mawr College scholar, ends her doctoral studies in Germany to become the school's first headmistress. She is in her early 20s and has never taught in a school.

M. Carey Thomas

My one aim and concentrated purpose shall be and is to show that a woman can learn, can reason, can compete with men in the grand fields of literature and science.

M. Carey Thomas
From a journal entry at age 14

CREATING TRADITIONS

1900s

1908 basketball team

1900

School physician, Dr. Mary Sherwood, patents a custom desk and chair that promote proper posture, and she establishes a daily exercise program for each girl.

1901

The Bryn Mawr School challenges St. Timothy's School in basketball, winning 8–7. Boys are not allowed as spectators, and players' names are not permitted to be published.

1903

Mary Elizabeth Garrett clears and levels the fields at her Montebello estate for sports competition. Stables are converted to showers and dressing rooms.

1904

A major Exhibition of Gymnasium Works is performed by the girls at school. The very first "exhibitions," precursors to Gym Drill, may have been performed as early as 1896.

1906

Often referred to as a bold "experiment in education," The Bryn Mawr School has nearly 300 girls enrolled.

1910

Edith Hamilton creates The Bryn Mawr School League, a service association for alumnae. League members teach academics and practical skills at the YWCA for many years. The league extends its community service by partnering with the Red Cross during World War I.

1912

Bryn Mawr builds an open-air classroom in the corner of the cement courtyard at Cathedral Street. Even though the traffic, noise, and soot are unrelenting, "fresh-air" learning persists for the next ten years. Each student receives a blanket to keep warm. Bryn Mawr acquires a playing field nearby for basketball and field hockey. The field, however, is not regulation size.

Millicent Carey, Class of 1916

1914

Edith Hamilton chooses as the first Bryn Mawr School uniform a dark blue serge with a full skirt. In the spring, a lighter and cooler blue linen is worn.

1915

Mary Elizabeth Garrett, the benefactress of The Bryn Mawr School, Bryn Mawr College, and Johns Hopkins Medical School, dies on April 3, leaving the bulk of her estate to M. Carey Thomas to administer. The conditions of her will firmly establish Bryn Mawr as a girls' college-preparatory school.

Girls in the first school uniform

Balance beam exercise during Gym Drill

EDUCATING GIRLS

1916

World War I brings economic challenges to Baltimore, and schools are asked to operate four instead of five days a week. Miss Hamilton observes that as "the fires are already stoked in the furnaces," lessons at Bryn Mawr would continue on Saturdays.

1917

Bryn Mawr purchases land on Brevard Street, providing outdoor sports fields next to the school. Montebello is primarily used for weekend trips for students and teachers to enjoy time outside of the city.

1918

Dr. Mary Sherwood is forced to close the school during the influenza epidemic. Bryn Mawr students who are well enough to study continue their lessons, thanks to their teachers, who deliver work to their homes.

1920

Increasing enrollment requires the purchase of another building for the Primary at Cathedral Street, which includes classrooms and a music room.

> All things should be called into question.
>
> *Edith Hamilton*

1921

Because of inflation caused by World War I, tuition has almost doubled in six years, rising from $250 in 1915 to $400. Many families are struggling financially.

1922

Citing health reasons, Edith Hamilton resigns as the first headmistress of The Bryn Mawr School. Students and families are heartbroken when she leaves. The Alumnae Association establishes a scholarship in her name and commissions her portrait, which now hangs in the Edith Hamilton Library.

Cathedral Street School

MOVING TO MELROSE

Amy Kelly, associate professor of English at Wellesley College, succeeds Edith Hamilton as Bryn Mawr's second headmistress.

Students begin playing field hockey at Mt. Washington. According to the *Bryn Mawrtyr*, "every now and then a girl received a black eye or had her front teeth knocked out."

1923

Bryn Mawr School founder M. Carey Thomas, recently retired president of Bryn Mawr College, makes national news when the League of Women Voters recognizes her as one of the twelve "greatest living American women."

1924

Rosabelle Sinclair, a graduate of St. Leonard's School in Scotland, where girls' lacrosse originated, joins the school's Athletic Department. By the spring of 1925, girls are throwing lacrosse balls for distance as a field day event and organizing into teams for play in the following year. In the first interscholastic game in 1927, Bryn Mawr prevails 13 to 1 against Friends School.

1928

The Cathedral Street school is overcrowded with 350 students, and the area is becoming increasingly congested by traffic and pollution. Families are moving out of the city, and private schools are following them, marking the beginning of the country school movement. In the spring, Headmistress Amy Kelly announces plans to acquire the 26-acre Gordon family property on Melrose Avenue, and a fund-raising campaign is launched to raise $300,000 for the purchase. In the fall, school opens with the Primary School (K–Grade 4) and Main I (Grade 5) on the new campus.

1930

A campus plan echoing Thomas Jefferson's design for the University of Virginia is created, but it is never fully implemented due to the Depression. The first buildings on Melrose Avenue will be self-sufficient and fireproof and will surround an open common area.

Edith Hamilton's first book, *The Greek Way*, is published.

1931

Mains II and III (Grades 6 and 7) move into the new Garrett Building. Girls in the upper grades continue to attend classes at Cathedral Street in the morning, and they travel to the country campus on Melrose Avenue each afternoon for study hall and athletics.

The Gordon Building, 1928

Amy Kelly

Margaret Hamilton

Elizabeth Thomas

Janet Howell Clark

Katharine Van Bibber

1932

Headmistress Kelly is granted a year's sabbatical to continue research on her book. *Eleanor of Aquitaine and the Four Kings*, published by Harvard University Press in 1950, is still considered an important biography of the queen. Margaret Hamilton (Edith Hamilton's sister), and Elizabeth Thomas lead the school during the sabbatical year.

The Parents' Association opens a thrift shop for families to buy used uniforms, books, and "extra-curricula impedimenta."

1933

Amy Kelly resigns to return to Wellesley College, and Margaret Hamilton serves the school as headmistress until 1935. In the summer, Bryn Mawr purchases a prefabricated building from the Episcopal Cathedral of the Incarnation and transports it to campus, permitting the remaining classes to move from Cathedral Street.

1935

Bryn Mawr celebrates fifty years and marks the end of the Cathedral Street era. M. Carey Thomas and longtime school physician Mary Sherwood die, and Margaret Hamilton retires after 31 years at the school.

Janet Howell Clark , Class of 1906, becomes the third headmistress of the school. Dr. Clark is a Bryn Mawr College alumna and holds a doctorate in physics from Johns Hopkins University. She has taught at Bryn Mawr College and Smith College, and she specialized in biophysics and ultra-violet radiation at the Johns Hopkins School of Hygiene and Public Health for seventeen years.

1938–1939

Dr. Clark leaves Bryn Mawr to become the dean of women and head of the Department of Physics at the University of Rochester. Elizabeth Thomas serves again as interim headmistress until Katharine Van Bibber, Class of 1920, can leave her position at The Brearley School to become the school's fourth headmistress.

Scarf Dance
Valerie Penrose Hodges,
and Alice Kimberly Wolf,
Class of 1932

50 YEARS

1940

Students form the Christian Association to sponsor domestic and international service projects as well as school speakers. Students assemble and ship packages of food and clothing to families in war-torn Europe and help the Red Cross and the World Student Service Fund efforts. For many years, members are chosen to attend the Buck Hill Falls Conference to share ideas with other students.

1941

The Bryn Mawr School Bulletin records — "On the eighth of December, the day after Pearl Harbor, the Bryn Mawr School, excused from classes, sat on the floor of the gymnasium in utter silence to hear the President [on the radio] ask Congress to declare war on Japan. At the end of the speech, the School rose with solemn faces for the 'Star-Spangled Banner,' and then filed, still silent, back to its lessons."

1942–1946

Bryn Mawr students learn first aid and Red Cross training and join the Inter-High School Congress to coordinate war work in the city, sell war bonds and stamps, count tires, roll bandages, work in the Bendix plant in the summers, and plant victory gardens. Many alumnae are overseas driving ambulances and working in hospitals and clinics.

GROWING AS A SCHOOL

1946

After the Glee Club's production of *Trial by Jury*, the faculty surprises the school by taking the stage in student uniforms and tunics to perform a full-length parody of the Gilbert and Sullivan play.

1948

The Parents' Association establishes the first spring Bazaar to raise money for the school's building fund and holds the first of many annual father-daughter dinners.

1949

The new Elizabeth Thomas Auditorium also serves as the school's gymnasium, cafeteria, and kitchen. Renovations to the Garrett Building improve the school's science laboratories, ease scheduling conflicts, and allow art history, Bible studies, and economics to be introduced into the curriculum.

1950

The Parents' Music Committee raises funds to help sponsor the Young Musician Series, which brings professional musicians, dancers, and performers to Bryn Mawr and other area independent schools.

School enrollment reaches 406 students.

The Mary Elizabeth Garrett Building

1951

Bryn Mawr continues to grow with the addition of an art studio and a complete renovation of the Gordon Building. A "Sustaining Fund" is established to develop resources "to pay better salaries, to give scholarships, and to put something aside for capital improvements," as well as to establish the first annual giving program.

In the fall, members of the Bryn Mawr Dramatic Club invite the Dramatic Association of Gilman School to join them in a program of two one-act plays.

1953–1955

The school library is reorganized, and the number of volumes increases from 1,500 to more than 5,000 cataloged books.

The new Margaret Hamilton Building relieves crowding in Garrett and the Gatehouse, and covered walkways connect the Gatehouse to the Elizabeth Thomas Auditorium. The music room, with its several small practice areas, enlarges the art studio.

1962

The Bryn Mawr School Board of Managers votes that, effective September 1963, "All fully qualified applicants will be considered for admission to The Bryn Mawr School regardless of color."

Katharine Van Bibber retires after twenty-three years of leading Bryn Mawr. The school names the new gymnasium in her honor and awards her the hockey-basketball-lacrosse pin and a silver cup—the equivalent of a Gym Drill bar—for her years of service.

INSPIRING INTELLECTUAL CURIOSITY

1963

Diane Howell, formerly of the Winsor School and Milton Academy, becomes headmistress.

Mélange, the Upper School literary magazine, debuts.

mélange
1963
a magazine of creative writing

bryn mawr school
baltimore, maryland
volume 1   no. 1

1969

The first Senior Projects provide students an opportunity to explore specific areas of interest.

1972

Bryn Mawr's new Lower School complex is under construction, and the revolutionary, open-space design by noted architect Marcel Breuer brings a new approach to the education of younger students. Trustee Edith Hooper is quoted in *The Sun* that the intention is to build a Lower School that is "utterly adjustable to the future."

1973

Blair D. Stambaugh becomes headmistress upon Diane Howell's retirement. The newly established Middle School is directed by Janet Barnitz. A formal coordinated Upper School academic program begins with Gilman School.

The Cathedral Street building is demolished to make way for the Meyerhoff Symphony Hall. Bryn Mawr alumnae salvage a large mosaic with the school's name that will be installed under a portico at the Melrose Avenue campus.

1975

Bryn Mawr adopts a new school uniform, providing students with more green and yellow apparel choices, including a blazer and a plaid kilted skirt.

1977

Bryn Mawr Little School opens in the Gordon Building Annex, providing a coeducational childcare and preschool program for children of working women. A second Little School program operates from 1983–1988 on the Goucher College campus. In 1989, the two Little School programs consolidate on the Melrose Avenue campus in a new building erected on the site of the Old Study Hall.

Barbara Landis Chase becomes headmistress at Bryn Mawr after leaving the Wheeler School. Her predecessor, Blair D. Stambaugh, departs Bryn Mawr to head the Baldwin School.

83

Bryn Mawr inaugurates its technology initiative by cosponsoring Microfest with the Apple Computer company. The school also provides adult computer classes and a summer camp program for girls in science and technology.

19

The school celebrates its centennial year and is recognized by the U.S. Department of Education and the Council of American Private Schools as an exemplary school.

100 Years

Diane Howell

Blair D. Stambaugh

Barbara Landis Chase

DEVELOPING MIND, BODY, & SPIRIT

1986

A forty-hour service requirement is put in place for graduation.

The school's music program and the Lower School art program move into the newly renovated Music and Arts Center, adjacent to the Gordon Building.

1987

Centennial Hall opens and is dedicated by cutting a giant ribbon and launching yellow balloons.

Centennial Hall ribbon-cutting

1989

Bryn Mawr creates a Multicultural Committee to provide a forum for conversations and activities related to the community's various cultures and ethnicities.

The school hosts its first summer Reader's Camp to encourage a love of books and build strong reading skills for young school-aged children from Baltimore City.

The first athletics Booster's Club is formed; and dance becomes a varsity sport.

1991

Dayseye performs the American and British national anthems at a baseball game attended by President George Bush and Queen Elizabeth II at Baltimore's Memorial Stadium.

Art Council is created to work alongside Bryn Mawr's Athletic Association and Student Government Association.

1993

Rosabelle Sinclair, who brought the sport of girl's lacrosse to The Bryn Mawr School and to America, is the first woman inducted into the National Lacrosse Hall of Fame.

The Barbara Landis Chase Dance Studio and Mildred Natwick Lobby of Centennial Hall, designed by Cho Wilks and Benn, receive a Grand Design Award from the American Institute of Architects.

The new Edith Hamilton Library opens in the recently renovated Howell Center.

1994

Barbara Landis Chase leaves Bryn Mawr to become the first female head of Phillips Academy, Andover. Former Bryn Mawr teacher and administrator Bodie Brizendine returns to serve as interim headmistress. Seventy-minute class periods are introduced in the Upper School to provide for in-depth class discussions and special activity periods.

Bodie Brizendine

1995

Dr. Rebecca MacMillan Fox becomes headmistress at Bryn Mawr, after serving as a dean at William Smith College and an assistant dean at Bryn Mawr College.

Dr. Rebecca MacMillan Fox

1996

Senior Exit Interviews are held for the first time, allowing students to give feedback to the school on their educational experience.

A Peer Education Program is instituted, bringing Bryn Mawr Upper School students together with fifth-grade girls to discuss effective and appropriate ways to address challenges at school and in life.

1997

The 25th anniversary of the opening of the Lower School is celebrated by dedicating the new Lower School Science Center. Students watch as work begins on the DNA molecule climber that is being built on the playground.

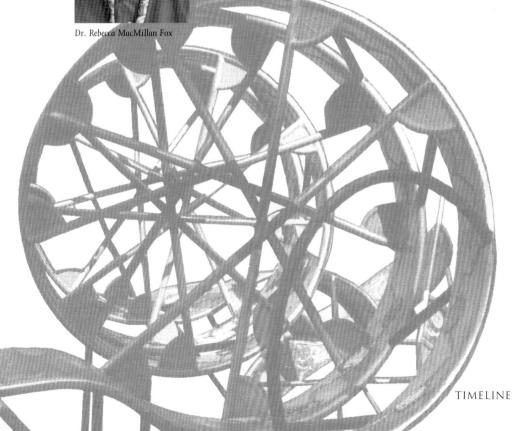

LEADING CONSIDERED & CONSEQUENTIAL LIVES

1998

After decades of renting playing fields at the Mt. Washington Club, Bryn Mawr purchases the property, gaining a lighted playing field, a clubhouse, and space for meetings and events.

1999

Bryn Mawr is designated a Governor's Green School just one year after launching "Stewardship 2000: Bryn Mawr's Environmental Initiative for the 21st Century."

The Edith Hamilton Scholars Program is established to provide seniors an opportunity to pursue a unique course of independent study outside the framework of the formal classroom.

The Julia Clayton Baker Chair in Environmental Stewardship is established as the school advances studies and work on campus around environmental issues.

2001

A Bryn Mawr School Master Plan is completed. Pedestrian bridges are built to connect three co-ordinated campuses–Bryn Mawr, Gilman, and Roland Park Country Schools.

Rebecca MacMillan Fox leaves Bryn Mawr to join

the administration at the University of Rochester. Alumna Katy Dallam takes leave from her teaching duties at Harford Day School to become interim headmistress.

Katy Dallam

2002

Maureen E. Walsh becomes headmistress. She is the former head of the Lower School at Poly Prep Country Day School in Brooklyn, New York.

2004

Bryn Mawr's Centennial Gym Drill is celebrated with reenactments from the programs of earlier years.

Students, mentored by teacher, coach, and administrator Jeanette Budzik, create a documentary video combining archival photography and alumnae interviews.

Maureen E. Walsh at the North Building ribbon-cutting ceremony

2006

The new 28,000-square-foot North Building features state-of-the-art science laboratories, a dance studio, music practice rooms, computer and language laboratories, and classrooms with Harkness tables to facilitate student-directed discussions.

2009

The Bryn Mawr School Board of Trustees approves "Vision 2020: Bryn Mawr in the 21st Century," which will serve as a guide to decision-making in key areas of school planning and operation for the next decade.

2010

Bryn Mawr celebrates its 125th anniversary year, honoring the vision of the school's founders and reaffirming the strengths of an education for girls.

125 YEARS

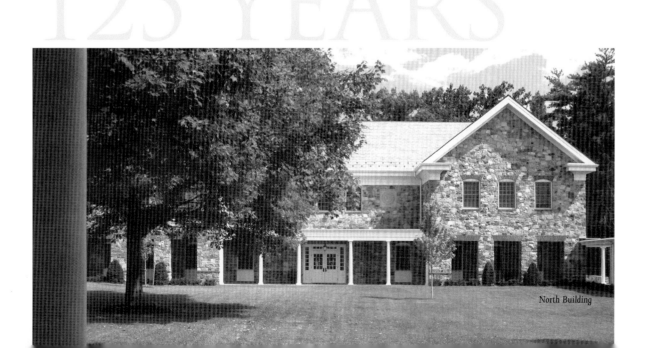

North Building

NOTES

Unless noted otherwise, the following documents can be found in the Archives Collection of The Bryn Mawr School.

CHAPTER ONE

[1] *The Harvard University Catalog, 1879–1880*, Charles W. Sever publisher, Cambridge, MA, 1879. 221.

[2] Sander, Kathleen Waters. *Mary Elizabeth Garrett: Society and Philanthropy in the Gilded Age.* Baltimore: Johns Hopkins University Press, 2008. 50.

[3] Chase, Barbara L. "M. Carey Thomas and the 'Friday Night': A Case Study in Female Social Networks and Personal Growth." Master's thesis, Johns Hopkins University, 1990.

[4] Marjorie Housepian Dobkin, ed., *The Making of a Feminist: Early Journals and Letters of M. Carey Thomas*, Kent, Ohio: Kent State University Press, 1979.

[5] Horowitz, Helen Lefkowitz. *The Power and Passion of M. Carey Thomas.* New York: Alfred A. Knopf, 1994. 228.

[6] Letter, Marion Talbot to M. Carey Thomas, January 12, 1885.

[7] Letter, Mary Elizabeth Garrett to Edith Hamilton, May 15, 1897.

[8] See Pokempner, Elizabeth, "'Unusual Qualifications': Teachers at the Bryn Mawr School, 1885-1901" in *Maryland Historical Magazine*, Vol. 93, No. 1 (Spring1998). 77-87.

[9] Catalog, The Bryn Mawr School, 1885. 2-3.

[10] Catalog, The Bryn Mawr School, 1885. 2-3.

[11] Letter, Edith Hamilton to M. Carey Thomas, February 5, 1915.

[12] Clarke, Dr. Edward H., *Sex in Education; or, A Fair Chance for Girls.* Boston: James R. Osgood and Company. 1875. 127.

[13] "Present Tendencies in Women's Colleges and University Education," address delivered by M. Carey Thomas at the Quarter-Centennial Meeting of the Association of College Alumnae, Boston, November 6, 1907. 69.

[14] The Friends Academy had been established by the Orthodox Quakers Dr. James Carey Thomas and Francis T. King to provide a Quaker education for their children in 1870, and was moved into this building in 1875.

[15] Cadwalader, Mary H., "No Carpet and No Red Door, The Bryn Mawr School Stood for Brains," *Baltimore Evening Sun*, December 2, 1972.

[16] Calculated through www.measuringworth.com, a service provided by leading economists from the University of Illinois.

[17] Pompeiian bricks were half the height of standard bricks and had metal chips embedded in the clay which turned black after firing, giving a rugged, aged appearance to the brown tones of the brick.

[18] "A Study in Brown: the Bryn Mawr School Building, Cathedral and Preston Streets." *The Baltimore Sun.* June 12, 1890. 6.

[19] Dr. Dudley Allen Sargent, director of the Hemenway Gymnasium at Harvard from 1879 to 1919, introduced there his theories of building muscle tone through measurement and prescribed exercises on machines he designed to improve the health and physical capabilities of any person. He described his work in "The Apparatus of the Hemenway Gymnasium," *The Harvard Register*, January 1880. 45: "Each is designed to bring into action one or more sets of muscles, and all can be adjusted to the capacity of a child or of an athlete." He trained several hundred men and women in physical education at his Sargent School of Physical Training in Cambridge, Massachusetts, (Leonard, p. 100), which, in 1929, became part of Boston University and is now the Boston University College of Rehabilitation Sciences: Sargent College.

[20] "A Study in Brown: the Bryn Mawr School Building, Cathedral and Preston Streets." *The Baltimore Sun.* June 12, 1890. 6.

[21] "Early Morning Fire." *The Baltimore Sun.* October 7, 1892. 8.

[22] There is a set of detailed inventory books of the artwork in the Cathedral Street building in the school archives.

[23] Bull, Lucy. "A Model School in Baltimore." Critic. December 3, 1894. 398.

24 Baedeker, Karl. *The United States with an Excursion into Mexico: Handbook for Travelers*. 2nd ed. New York: Charles Scribner's Sons, 1899. 272.

25 In Sander, p. 157, Daniel Coit Gilman to Charles Gwinn and George Dobbin, "Dear Sirs," November 9, 1888, Box 507277, Alan Mason Chesney Medical Archives of the Johns Hopkins Medical Institutions.

26 "The Great Hospital." *The Baltimore Sun*. May 8, 1889. 5.

27 Later called the Women's Medical School Fund, Sander, 170.

28 *Finding Aid to the Francis T. King Reminiscences*, Ms. 322, Special Collections, Milton S. Eisenhower Library, The Johns Hopkins University.

29 "The Medical School." *Baltimore Sun* February 23, 1893. 7.

30 Sander, 185.

31 "The Medical School." *Baltimore Sun* February 23, 1893. 7.

32 Miers, Michael, ed. "A Chronology of Major Dates in the Life and Philanthropy of Mary Elizabeth Garrett." *Celebrating the Philanthropy of Mary Elizabeth Garrett, Champion of Women in Medicine*. The Alan Mason Chesney Medical Archives of the Johns Hopkins Medical Institutions, n.d. Web. March 22, 2010.

33 Sander, 204.

CHAPTER TWO

1 See the volume of correspondence 1885–1896, in the school archives collection in which the founders oversee the hanging of maps, the purchase of coal, the management of staff, parents, and faculty, etc.

2 *The Bryn Mawr School Catalogs*, 1885–1895. 2.

3 McIntosh, Millicent Carey, address, "Opening assembly on the 75th anniversary celebration of The Bryn Mawr School," November 4, 1960, as published in *The Bryn Mawr School Bulletin*, Vol. XVII, No. 1, 1960–1961. 7.

4 Letters, Francis T. King and M. Carey Thomas 1885–1890.

5 Letter, John G. Johnson to M. Carey Thomas, June 12,1911, in which the attorney explains the detail of past contracts with Edith Hamilton.

6 Hallett, Judith P. "Edith Hamilton (1867–1963)." *Classical World*. 90.2/3 (1996–1997). 109.

7 Davis, Nancy, and Barbara Donahue, *Miss Porter's School: A History*. Miss Porter's School, Farmington, CT. 1992. 5.

8 *Program of the Bryn Mawr College*, 1905–06. 172.

9 *The Bryn Mawr School Catalog*, 1895–1896. 3.

10 Alice would become the first female professor at Harvard Medical School, take an integral part in Jane Addam's Hull House in Chicago, and be noted as a pioneer in workplace related disease.

11 Singer, Sandra L. *Adventures Abroad: North American Women at German-Speaking Universities*, 1868-1915. Westport, CT: Praeger Publishers. 2003. 74. Hamilton, Alice. Exploring the Dangerous Trades: the Autobiography of Alice Hamilton, M.D. Boston: Little, Brown and Company. 1943. 44-45.

12 Hamilton, Alice, article in *Atlantic Monthly*, 1965, quoted in Reid, Doris Fielding. *Edith Hamilton: An Intimate Portrait*. New York: W.W. Norton & Company.1967. 36.

13 Hamilton, Edith, address, "Opening assembly on the 75th anniversary celebration of The Bryn Mawr School," November 4, 1960, as published in *The Bryn Mawr School Bulletin*," Vol. XVII, No. 1, 1960–1961. 28.

14 Correspondence between Edith Hamilton, Mary Elizabeth Garrett, and M. Carey Thomas, 1915-1920.

15 McIntosh, Millicent Carey. *The Bryn Mawr School Bulletin*. 1960-1961. 8. The Bible passage is Philippians 4:8.

16 Branham, Grace, "A Tribute," in *The Bryn Mawr School Alumnae Bulletin*. 1958–1959. 4.

17 Ibid.

18 Hamilton, Edith, "A Message" in *The Bryn Mawr School Alumnae Bulletin*. 1958-1959. 4.

19 Ibid. 11.

20 Anne Kinsolving Brown, Class of 1924, "Address to the alumnae," April,1947. Manuscript.

21 The meetings were covered in a variety of *Baltimore Sun* articles, including "To Plan Suffrage Fight," January 7, 1910. 14; "'Tis Suffragists' Great Day," February 13, 1912. 12; "Suffragists Meet Today," March 29, 1912. 10.

NOTES

22 *Bryn Mawtyr* 1910-1925, as well as numerous *Sun* articles, provide details of this involvement.

23 Letter, Edith Hamilton to M. Carey Thomas, March 16, 1914.

24 Ibid.

25 Letter, Edith Hamilton to M. Carey Thomas, November 23, 1920.

26 Unidentified newspaper article.

27 "Garrett Millions to Miss Thomas." *New York Times* April 9, 1915. 6.

28 Klein, Abbe' Felix. *In the Land of Strenuous Living.* Chicago. A.C. McClurg & Co. 1905. 318-320. "'Prep' School for Girls Planned" *The San Francisco Call.* April 21, 1910. 9.

29 Letter, Diane Howell to Janice Proctor, September 9, 1967; Doris Fielding Reid to Mrs. Arthur U. Hooper, August 18, 1969.

CHAPTER THREE

1 Letter, "To the Parents and Alumnae of The Bryn Mawr School" from M. Carey Thomas, March 19, 1926. From 1924 to 1927, Amy Kelly would take short leaves from the school to assist a committee that was establishing a new kind of women's college in Bennington, Vermont, based in large part on her research, elaborated in Kelly, Amy. *A Curriculum to Build a Mental World: A Proposal for a College of Liberal Arts for Women.* The Bryn Mawr School, Baltimore, MD. 1927.

2 Letter.

3 M. Carey Thomas was a member of the College Board, serving as a vice chair from 1900-1902. VanOverbeke, Marc A. *The Standardization of American Schooling: Linking Secondary and Higher Education, 1870-1910.* New York, NY: Palgrave MacMillan, 2008. 151-152.

4 Jacobs, Bradford McE. *Gilman Walls Will Echo: The Story of the Gilman Country School, 1897-1947.* Baltimore, MD: Waverly Press. 1947.

5 Bowditch, Eden Unger. *Growing Up in Baltimore: A Photographic History.* Charleston, SC: Arcadia Publishing, 2001. 47.

6 Esslinger, Dean R. *Friends for Two Hundred Years: A History of Baltimore's Oldest School.* Baltimore, MD: Friends School. 1983.

7 "Bryn Mawr School Going to Suburbs." *Sun.* March 9, 1928. 3.

8 *Bryn Mawr School Alumnae Semi-Annual Bulletin,* No. 2, January 1928. 1.

9 *The Bryn Mawr School Alumnae Semi-Annual Bulletin,* No. 1, May 1928. 1.

10 "Bryn Mawr to Conduct Class at Two Places." *Sun.* September 25, 1930. 3.

11 Amy Kelly. *Bryn Mawr School Alumnae Annual Bulletin.* May 1933. 2.

12 "The Mary Garrett Building." *The Bryn Mawr School Alumnae Annual Bulletin.* May, 1932. 2.

13 "Old Parish House Is Sold," *Sun,* June 3, 1933. 3.

14 Margaret Hamilton. *Bryn Mawr School Alumnae Annual Bulletin.* May 1934. 1.

15 "Fire Sweeps Roland Park Institution." *The Baltimore Sun.* June 5, 1947. 32.

16 "Five Firemen Injured in School Blaze." *The Baltimore Sun.* June 18, 1947. 28.

17 "Editorial." *The Bryn Mawr School Alumnae Annual Bulletin.* No. 9. May 1936. 1.

18 "Editorial." *The Bryn Mawr School Alumnae Annual Bulletin.* No. 11. May 1938. 1.

19 *The Bryn Mawr School Alumnae Annual Bulletin.* April 1941. 19.

20 "Editorial." *The Bryn Mawr School Alumnae Annual Bulletin.* No. 11. May 1938. 1.

21 "Miss Van Bibber is Appointed Head of Bryn Mawr School." *Sun.* December 17, 1938. 10.

CHAPTER FOUR

1 Transcript of interview with Katharine Van Bibber, undated, held sometime after 1988.

2 "Miss Edith Hamilton," *The Bryn Mawr School Bulletin.* 1960-1961. 29.

3 Ibid.

4 Van Bibber, Katharine. "From the Headmistress." *Bryn Mawr: Newsletter of the Bryn Mawr School.* March 1986. 1.

5 Ibid.

6 *The Bryn Mawr School Alumnae Bulletin.* May 1940. 2.

7 Ibid. 3.

8 *The Bryn Mawr School Alumnae Bulletin.* April 1941. 1.

9 Ibid.

10 Hanson, F. Allan. *Testing: Social Consequences of the Examined Life.* Berkeley: University of California Press, 1993. 213-217. http://ark.cdlib.org/ark:/13030/ft4m3nb2h2/.

11 "Preparedness in the Bryn Mawr School" in *The Bryn Mawr School Alumnae Annual Bulletin.* May 1942. 1-4.

12 *The Bryn Mawr School Alumnae Bulletin.* August 1950. 5.

13 "Summer Jobs." *The Quill.* June 10, 1943. 2-3.

14 "The Bryn Mawr School Today." *The Bryn Mawr School Alumnae Annual Bulletin.* May 1943. 4.

15 *The Bryn Mawr School Alumnae Bulletin.* May 1944. 3.

16 *The Bryn Mawr School Alumnae Bulletin.* May 1941. 6.

17 *The Bryn Mar School Alumnae Bulletin.* May 1946. 11. Bernstein, Barton J. "The Removal of War Production Board Controls on Business, 1944-1946." *The Business History Review.* Vol. 39, No. 2 (Summer 1965) 243-260.

18 *The Bryn Mawr School Alumnae Bulletin.* May 1947. 5.

19 "The Closing Chapter." *The Sun.* June 21, 1951. 12.

20 *The Bryn Mawr School Alumnae Bulletin.* May 1951. 3.

21 "Disguised as a Woman." *Burlington, Iowa Gazette.* December 5, 1900. "Donned Female Attire." *Baltimore News.* December 4, 1900.

22 "Old Marston School and Its Boys." *The Sun.* September 19, 1948. SM2.

23 *The Bryn Mawr School Alumnae Bulletin.* May 1951. 19.

24 *The Bryn Mawr School Alumnae Bulletin.* Winter 1953. 6.

25 *The Bryn Mawr School Bulletin.* 1956. 4.

26 *The Bryn Mawr School Bulletin.* 1957. 3.

27 Ibid. 18.

28 Ibid. 18.

29 *The Bryn Mawr School Bulletin.* 1958. 9.

30 Elizabeth Millspaugh and Katharine Van Bibber to the Parents, Alumnae and Friends of the School. January 30, 1962.

31 *The Bryn Mawr School Bulletin.* 1961-1962. 3.

CHAPTER FIVE

1 "New Head Named for Bryn Mawr." *Baltimore Sun.* December 26 1961. 26.

2 *The Bryn Mawr School Alumnae Bulletin,* 1961-1962. 11.

3 Woodring, Paul. "Challenging the Axioms." *The Saturday Review of Literature.* April 20, 1963. Reprinted in *The Bryn Mawr School Alumnae Bulletin,* Summer 1964. 9. See also Woodring, Paul. *Investment in Innovation: An Historical Appraisal of the Fund for the Advancement of Education.* Boston: Little, Brown and Co. 1970.

4 *The Bryn Mawr School Alumnae Bulletin,* 1962-1963. 5.

5 Henry, Helen. "New Horizons Opened for Negro Children." *Baltimore Sun.* March 28, 1965. C1.

6 *Communiqué.* Spring 1973. 20.

7 Howell, Diane. "The Freedom of the Independent School." *The Bryn Mawr School Bulletin.* Winter 1965. 3-5.

8 Fine, Dr. Benjamin. "Private Schools are Booming." *The Sun.* September 12, 1965. F34.

9 Clarke, Gerald. "Enrollment of Negroes Shows Rise." *The Sun.* January 4, 1965. 32.

10 Clarke, Gerald. "Need for Teachers Acute, Dr. Sensenbaugh Stresses." *The Sun.* January 11, 1965. 36.

11 "Text of the President's Message to Congress on Education." *The Washington Post.* January 13, 1965. A10.

12 "Off and Running." *The Bryn Mawr School Bulletin.* Summer 1966. 3.

13 Howell, Diane. "The Library–A Wellspring." *The Bryn Mawr School Bulletin.* Summer 1967. 2-6.

14 "Independent Schools Share Common Spirit." *The Sun.* May 23, 1971. ED7.

15 *Bryn Mawr Newsletter.* May 1983. 1. *Quill.* May 1969. Vol XLVIII No 4. 4.

16 "Student Exchange." *The Bryn Mawr School Bulletin.* Summer 1968. 6.

17 Wallace, Weldon. "Seniors Test In-The-World Jobs" *The Sun.* June 4, 1969. C6.

18 "Excerpts from Harvard Overseers' Interim Report." *New York Times* September 19, 1969. 28.

19 *The Quill.* November, 1969. Various articles.

NOTES

20 Birge, Sue Rose. "The Coeducational Trend in Higher Education." *The Bryn Mawr School Bulletin.* 1968-1969. 6.

21 Randall, Judith and James Walsh. "What Next: Selling Those ABC's." *The Sun.* July 6, 1969. TW7.

22 Jablow, Martha. "A Catholic School Still, Though the Nuns Have Gone." *The Sun.* October 8, 1972. C1.

23 Lehner, Urban C. "Breaking Tradition: Fighting to Stay Alive, Many Prep Schools Try To Change Their Image." *Wall Street Journal.* September 22, 1972. 1.

24 Hechinger, Fred M. "Choate and Rosemary Hall Will Merge in 1971." *New York Times.* September 25, 1968. 32.

25 Lehner.

26 "Last Drill Ends McDonogh's Military Look." *The Sun.* June 4, 1971. C20.

27 Howell, Diane. Report to the Board. March 9, 1971.

28 *The Bryn Mawr School Bulletin.* Winter 1971.

29 "A Building Is Educational, Too." *Baltimore Sun.* October 29, 1972. D1.

30 Grant, James. "Officials, Architectural Preservationists at Odds." *Baltimore Sun.* December 3, 1972. A22. Somerville, Frank P.L. "Does the State Really Care About Saving Landmarks?" *Baltimore Sun.* December 10, 1972. K1.

31 "Alumnae Salvage Mosaic." *The Quill.* Vol. LII, No. 3. March, 1973. 1.

32 *Communiqué.* Spring 1973. 3-4.

33 *Bryn Mawr Newsletter.* October 1989.

CHAPTER SIX

1 Bowler, Mike. "New England Teacher Chosen Headmistress of Bryn Mawr." *The Sun.* April 10, 1973. A13.

2 Letter, Dorothy J. Richardson to Diane Howell. September 8, 1972.

3 *Quill.* November 1972. Vol. LII, No. 1. 1.

4 *Quill.* June 1973. Vol. LII, No. 4. 1.

5 *Communiqué.* Summer 1978. 5.

6 *Special Report on Education.* World Book. 1973 ed.

7 "School Building, Enrollment Slump Expected." *The Sun.* August 17, 1973. C1.

8 Goldman, Daniel F. "Private Schools' New Man in Washington." *The Sun.* October 21, 1973. D1.

9 Bowler, Mike. "Private Colleges Seek Minority Aid." *The Sun.* December 6, 1975. B1.

10 *Communiqué.* Summer 1979. 192

11 *Communiqué:* Special Bryn Mawr Way Edition. March 1977. 2.

12 *Communiqué.* Spring/Summer 1977. 9.

13 *Communiqué.* Spring 1978. 3.

14 "Racial Isolation in Maryland Schools." *The Sun.* April 24, 1973. A14.

15 "City Enrollment Shrinking: School Figures Indicate Black Flight." *The Sun.* November 3, 1975. A1.

16 Arnett, Earl. "The Flow to Private School Increases." *The Sun.* November 28, 1977. B1.

17 *Communiqué.* March 1977.

18 "PAPAS, MSA, LRP Spell Evaluation for Bryn Mawr." *Communiqué.* Winter 1979. 1.

19 Ibid. 2.

20 "A Farewell to Bryn Mawr's Sixth Headmistress: Blair Danzoll Stambaugh." *Communiqué.* Summer 1980. 6-8.

CHAPTER SEVEN

1 Scott, Barbara F. "Private Schools' Public Concern." *New York Times.* September 6, 1981. A24.

2 "Recession Cuts Boarding School Role." *The New York Times.* December 1, 1982. B7.

3 Schwerzler, Nancy J. "50% Increase: Minority Enrollment in Private Schools Up." *The Sun.* September 6, 1981. A3. Low, Stuart. "Popularity Defies Price of Private Primary Schools." *The Sun.* October 25, 1981. AR1.

4 Chase, Barbara, letter to Bryn Mawr parents. February 3, 1981.

5 *Bryn Mawrtyr.* 1931. 50-51.

6 Rousuck, J. Wynn. "Private Schools for the Public?" *The Sun.* January 2, 1983. SM5.

7 *Bryn Mawr School Newsletter.* November 1982. 5.

8 "Goucher Students to Serve as Math Mentors" *Sun.* July 11, 1982. T15. "All-Girl Summer Camps Strive to Bridge the 'Computer Gap'" *Sun.* January 8, 1984. ED2.

9 Rehert, Isaac. "A Report Card's Out on High Schools and a Professor Gives Failing Grades." *The Sun*. November 7, 1984. 3B

10 "Here's to . . ." *The Sun*. June 10, 1984. E6.

11 *Bryn Mawr Newsletter*. April 1984.

12 *Bryn Mawr Newsletter*. June 1984.

13 Hochman, Anndee. "Foreign Languages Are Regaining Their Romance at Area High Schools." *The Washington Post*. May 18, 1986. C1.

14 *Bryn Mawr Newsletter*. Summer 1985.

15 *Communiqué*. Fall 1985.

16 *Bryn Mawr Newsletter*. March 1985.

17 Marquand, Robert. "Teacher Enthusiasm Fades in Fourth Year." *The Sun*. August 4, 1985. ET9.

18 Hawley, Jean. *Bryn Mawr Newsletter*. 1996.

19 Coalition of Essential Schools website, available May 2010 at http://www.essentialschools.org/.

20 *The Bryn Mawr School Annual Report*. 1986-1987. 4.

21 *Bryn Mawr Newsletter*. February 1987. 3.

22 *Bryn Mawr Newsletter*. November 1987. 2.

23 *Bryn Mawr Newsletter*. November 1987. 6.

24 *Bryn Mawr Newsletter*. Summer 1988.

25 Staples, Brent. "The Dwindling Black Presence on Campus." *New York Times*. April 27, 1986. SM46.

26 *Bryn Mawr Newsletter*. January/February 1992.

27 *Bryn Mawr Newsletter*. January/February 1993.

28 *The Bryn Mawr School Annual Report*. 1989-1990. 1-2.

29 *The Bryn Mawr School Annual Report*. 1991-1992. 27.

30 *The Bryn Mawr School Annual Report*. 1993-1994. 3-5.

31 "Private Schools Drawing More Pupils Despite Cost: Parents Dissatisfied with Public Schools." *The Sun*. December 27, 1991. 3A.

32 "Private-School Worries." *The Sun*. September 1, 1992.

33 *Bryn Mawr Newsletter*. December 1992/January 1993. 1. "Urban Landscape." *Sun*. October 29, 1992. 2C.

34 *Communiqué*. 1994. 3.

35 Gately, Gary. "Bryn Mawr Headmistress to lead Mass. Prep school." *The Sun*. February 23, 1994. 1B.

CHAPTER EIGHT

1 *Bryn Mawr Newsletter*. Fall 1994.

2 *Bryn Mawr Newsletter*. Winter 1994. 1.

3 *Bryn Mawr Newsletter*. May/June, 1995. 2.

4 *Bryn Mawr Newsletter*. February/March 1995. 1.

5 *Bryn Mawr Newsletter*. Spring 1996. 1.

6 McCraven, Marilyn and Mary Maushard. "Diversity at private schools is expanding." *The Sun*. December 2, 1996. 1B.

7 Bock, James. "MD schools face influx of students." *The Sun*. January 31, 1994. 1A.

8 Ibid.

9 Kaltenbach, Chris. "Parents fight for spot in 'right' school." *The Sun*. March 9, 1994. 1A.

10 Maushard, Mary. "Public's demand for private schools thriving in region." *The Sun*. March 26, 1996. 1A.

11 Kaufman, Jonathon. "Grade inflation: suburban parents shun many public schools, even the good ones." *The Wall Street Journal*. March 1, 1996. A1.

12 Maushard, Mary. "A month of hard decisions." *The Sun*. February 27, 1997. 1A.

13 Appleborne, Peter. "Record school enrollments, now and ahead." *The New York Times*. August 22, 1997. A14.

14 Maushard, Mary. "Building for the next 100 years." *The Sun*. June 7, 1996. 1A.

15 Maushard, Mary. "Building booms at private schools." *The Sun*. October 27, 1997. 1A.

16 *Bryn Mawr Newsletter*. April 1997. 2.

17 *The Bryn Mawr School Annual Report*. 1995-1996. 12.

18 "Private schools make run for real estate" *Baltimore Sun*. October 2, 1999. 1A.

19 *Bryn Mawr Newsletter*. Spring 2000. 1.

20 *Bryn Mawr Newsletter*. Summer 2001. 2. *The Bryn Mawr School Annual Report*. 1997-1998.

21 Golden, Daniel. "Paper Chase." *The Wall Street Journal*. January 23, 2001.

NOTES

22 Crossen, Cynthia. "Psychology of Spending." *The Wall Street Journal.* February 8, 2001. B1.

23 Kronholz, June. "Extracurricular Business." *The Wall Street Journal.* January 26, 2005. B1.

24 *Communiqué.* 2001. 3-5.

25 *Quill.* October 24, 2001. 1. *Bryn Mawr Newsletter.* Autumn 2001. 5.

26 Funk, David M., letter to the Bryn Mawr School Community, June 10, 2002.

27 *The Quill.* October 17, 2002. 4.

28 *Bryn Mawr Always Newsletter.* Spring 2008.

LEADERSHIP

1 Meigs, Cornelia. *What Makes a College?: A History of Bryn Mawr.* New York, NY: The Macmillan Company, 1956. 54.

2 Bucher, Nancy, SGA President, *Bryn Mawrtyr.* 1931. 73.

3 *Bryn Mawrtyr.* 1920. 36.

4 *Bryn Mawrtyr.* 1960. 46.

5 *The Bryn Mawr School Bulletin,* Winter 1965. 17.

6 *The Bryn Mawr School Bulletin.* Summer 1968. 12.

7 Solberg, Susan. "A Careful Approach to Service Learning in the Upper School." *Bryn Mawr School Newsletter.* Spring 1999. 2.

8 *Bryn Mawr Student Clubs and Organizations Handbook.* 2009-2010.

FINE & PERFORMING ARTS

1 Clements, Gabrielle DeV. "Fifteen Years of the Drawing Department of the Bryn Mawr School." *Bryn Mawrtyr.* 1931. 69-70.

2 "Girls at Bryn Mawr School Paint Original Pictures." *The Sunday Sun.* June 7, 1925. 3.

3 "Four School Groups Aiding in Museum Loan Campaign." *Sun.* October 20, 1924. 7.

4 McHold, Pat Fisher. "Eleanor Gibson Graham." *The Bryn Mawr School Faculty: A Centennial Tribute.* 1985. 11.

5 "Club Notes." *The Quill.* November 16, 1966. 2. "Goings On in Art Club." *The Quill.* February 1962. 4.

6 "Glee Club." *Bryn Mawrtyr.* 1960. 50.

7 "Bryn Mawrkings." *The Bryn Mawr School Newsletter.* April 1982. 2.

8 McCloskey, Karin. "Bells, Canterbury Choir Make Public Appearances." *The Quill.* December 1972. 4.

9 Myles-Hunkin, Andrea. "Quips From the Quill." *The Quill.* November 1975. 2.

10 "The Bryn Mawr School Dramatic Club." *The Sun.* March 4, 1893. 10.

11 Beirne, Rosamond Randall. *Let's Pick the Daisies: The History of the Bryn Mawr School, 1885–1967,* Baltimore: The Bryn Mawr School, 1970. 82.

12 *Bryn Mawrtyr.* 1931. 69.

13 "Girls to Give Shakespeare," *Sun,* April 7, 1910. 7.

14 "Dramatics." *Bryn Mawrtyr.* 1931. 64.

15 "Dramatics." *Bryn Mawrtyr.* 1917. 87.

16 "A Kiss for Cinderella." *The Quill.* March 20, 1924. 3-4. "Dramatics." *Bryn Mawrtyr* 1924. 64.

17 *The Quill.* February 1940. Vol. 18., No. 3. 1.

18 *The Bryn Mawr School Faculty: A Centennial Tribute.* 1985. 11.

19 "Operetta is Presented by Bryn Mawr Students." *The Sun.* March 31, 1928. 5. *Bryn Mawrtyr.* 1931.

20 "From the Greenroom." *Bryn Mawr School Bulletin.* May 1951. 19.

21 Schaenen, Inda. "At Bryn Mawr Chance to Dance Is Varsity Sport." *Bryn Mawr School Newsletter.* February 1989. 6. Reprinted from *The Baltimore Messenger.*

ATHLETICS

1 *The Bryn Mawrtyr.* 1950, 1960.

2 The girls at Bryn Mawr were considered "experts" in fencing as early as 1902. "Girls Form Fencing Club." *Sun.* December 23, 1902. 12.

3 Tanton, Bill. "A Tradition Worth Savoring." *The Evening Sun.* February 6, 1985. E1.

4 *The Bryn Mawr School Bulletin,* 1960–1961. p. 26.

5 "Hockey Society Fad Now." *The Sun.* October 28, 1911. 16.

6 *Bryn Mawrtyr.* 1923. 98.

7 *Bryn Mawrtyr.* 1924. 89.

8 *The Quill.* October, 1956. 5.

9 *The Quill.* March 22, 1925. 3.

[10] "Bryn Mawr Varies Sports." *The Sun.* September 28, 1930. S5.

[11] *Bryn Mawrtyr.* 1931. 53.

[12] Just, Kelly. "Bryn Mawr athletic teams expand." *The Quill.* October 25, 1989. 8.

[13] McCarty, Mary. "Gym Drill and Track Meets." *Bryn Mawrtyr.* 1931. 55.

[14] *Bryn Mawr School Newsletter.* October 1984. 7.

[15] *Bryn Mawr School Newsletter.* November 1989.

[16] Tapager, Cheri. "Tennis Adjusts to Fall." *The Quill.* October 25, 1989. 8.

[17] *The Bryn Mawr School Bulletin.* May 1947. 15.

[18] Calendar. *Bryn Mawr School Newsletter.* April 1988. 8.

[19] "Varsity Softball Starts First Season." *The Quill.* April 29, 1988. 4.

[20] *The Quill.* December 3, 1990. 3.

[21] "Bryn Mawr Golfers: Swinging into Action." *The Quill.* April 13, 2004. 8.

[22] *Bryn Mawr School Newsletter.* February 1985. 6.

[23] Hemmendinger, Julia. "We'll Always be the Mawrtians." *The Quill.* May 2007. 8.

Gym Drill & Banner March

[1] "Swimming and Fencing at Bryn Mawr." *The Sun.* May 13, 1893. 10.

[2] "Girl Athletes. Exhibition of Gymnasium Work at Bryn Mawr School." *Baltimore Evening News.* April 18, 1896.

[3] Beirne, 12-13. "History of the Bryn Mawr School." *Bryn Mawr School Bulletin.* 1960-1961. Randolph, Carmen Santos. "I Remember When…" *The Quill.* December 1956. 5.

[4] "Japan's Sons Greeted." *The Sun.* November 5, 1909. 14.

[5] "The Gymnasium Exhibition." *The Bryn Mawrtyr.* 1911. 74.

[6] Carey, Millicent. "The Gymnasium Exhibition." *The Bryn Mawrtyr.* 1915. 62. "The Gymnasium Exhibition." *The Bryn Mawrtyr.* 1916. 43.

[7] "The Gymnasium Exhibition of 1919." *The Bryn Mawrtyr.* 1920. 34-35.

[8] "The Gymnasium Exhibition." *The Bryn Mawrtyr.* 1922.

[9] Patton, Kathy. "A Look at the Gym Drill." *The Quill.* June, 1966. 1-2.

[10] Randall, Julia. "Bryn Mawr Brigadier." *The Quill.* February 1975. 3.

[11] "Gym Drill." *The Quill.* May 27, 1940. 1. Ibid. June 1965. 1.

[12] "Have You Heard?" *The Quill.* November 1968. 1.

[13] "Traditions Live On At Gym Drill." *The Quill.* May 4, 1990. 1.

[14] "Are We Really Strange?" *The Quill.* May 4, 1990. 3. "Should The Gym Drill Tradition Continue?" *The Quill.* June 7, 1990. 3.

[15] "Jammin' Gym Drill." *The Quill.* June 5, 1991. 8.

[16] *Bryn Mawrtyr Supplement.* 1995. 12.

[17] "Celebrating 100 Years of Gym Drill." *Communiqué.* 2004. 5.

Bazaar & Maypole

[1] Beirne. 99.

[2] "Bryn Mawr Bazaar Aids Building Fund." *Sun.* November 15, 1930. 3.

[3] *Bryn Mawr School Alumnae Association Bulletin.* 1948. 13.

Graduation

[1] "Bryn Mawr's First Diploma Day," *Sun,* June 9, 1893. 8.

[2] "Bryn Mawr School," *Sun,* June 9, 1894.

[3] "daisy." *Online Etymology Dictionary.* Douglas Harper, Historian. August 15, 2010. http://dictionary.reference.com/browse/daisy

[4] Jones, Nanette. "The Eye of the Day." *The Bryn Mawr School Newsletter.* December 1981. 1.

[5] Chase, Barbara. "From the Head-mistress." *The Bryn Mawr School Newsletter.* April 1987. 1.

Edith Hamilton

[1] "Edith Hamilton, Classicist Dies." *The New York Times.* June 1, 1963. 16.

[2] Brown, John Mason. "The Heritage of Edith Hamilton: 1867-1963." *The Saturday Review.* June 22, 1963. 16-17.

NOTES

TRADITIONS

[1] "Editorial." The Bryn Mawrtyr. 1909. 8.

[2] "Katharine Van Bibber." The Bryn Mawr School Faculty: A Centennial Tribute. 1985. 36.

[3] "Odds and Ends." The Bryn Mawr School Alumnae Bulletin. 1971. 23.

[4] The Bryn Mawr School Newsletter. December 1988. 3.

[5] Crawford, Elizabeth. The Women's Suffrage Movement: a reference guide, 1866-1928. Routledge, NY. 2001. 448.

[6] Advertisement. The Bryn Mawrtyr. 1933. 85.

[7] Bouton, Kathy, and Phyllis Gilbert. "School Ring Initiated by Main VI." The Quill. March 1963. 1.

[8] Wexler, Natalie. "Grade 4 Holds Exotic Fair." The Quill. June 1971. 2-3.

FACULTY PHOTO CAPTIONS

Page 179:

1. Carmen Santos Randolph, Class of 1913, prepares the faculty for the annual Faculty Skit, late 1950s
2. Faculty, 1961
3. Julia Parker, Rosabelle Sinclair, and Nina Adamovitch attend an Alumnae Reunion, 1960s
4. Jean Hawley, Little School Director, 1981
5. Mary Guion Williams Griepenkerl, Class of 1932, 1960s
6. Erna Schirokauer, 1980s

Page 180:

7. John Robinson, 1993
8. Diane Levine with senior Becky Morris and Trustee L. Patrick Deering, 1994

9. Lila Lohr, 1978
10. Mary McPherson and Norma Simmons, 1982
11. Cornelia Donner, 1982
12. Centennial faculty, 1985

Page 181:

13. Dave Stephens, 1998
14. Jane Buxton Brown, Class of 1953, teaching Little School science, 1991
15. Alumnae/Faculty and Staff, 2005
16. Dorothy Clayborne, 1990s
17. Susan Reid Mills and Bobbie Miyasaki, 2010
18. Elaine Swyryn, 1996

Page 182:

19. Jackie Sanders, 1996
20. Jerry Brown goes for the block in the annual Student-Faculty basketball game as Bill Waters, Thanasi Letras, Justin Curtis, Brenda Wilson, Joanne Cho, Emma Bartlett, and Kris Schaffner look on, 2009–2010
21. Arna Margolis, 1987
22. Anne Eggleston Broadus, Class of 1988, 2008
23. Pat Nothstein, 1996
24. Bill Waters, 2010
25. Sallilynch Currin Smith, Class of 1958, 2009
26. Middle School Faculty, 2007
27. Emily Letras, 2010

Page 183:

28. Mary Armstrong Shoemaker, Class of 1969, 2006
29. Bryn Mawr's coaching staff, 2010
30. Practicing for the faculty skit, (L to R) Jeannette Budzik, Jenniffer Gray, Jason George, Wendy Kridel, Molly Smith, Joanne Cho, Lee Kladky (hidden), Vicky Mermelstein, and Emily Tankersley, 2007–2008
31. Upper School faculty, from top center: Steve Amann, Mary Beth Kircher, Liz Priest, Mary Armstrong Shoemaker, Class of 1969, Kris Schaffner, Class of 1993, Heather Wilson, David Alexander, Bob Aronstam, Dave Stephens, and Amanda Mann
32. Little School teacher Farzana Muqueeth receives her laptop from Director of Technology Lynn Byank, 2003

PHOTOGRAPHY

The following images were loaned to Bryn Mawr by other institutions:

Courtesy of the Bryn Mawr College Library, Special Collections: viii and 188: The Five Founders by N. H. Busey, and 4UL: Mamie Gwinn by Maler Buchner, Stuttgart, Germany

Courtesy of the Guilford College Archives: 4LL, Bessie King

Courtesy of the Goucher College Archives: 4LR, Julia Rogers

Courtesy of the Johns Hopkins University Archives: 6

Courtesy of the Yale University Archives: 166L

There are several hundred thousand images in the archives collection, many of which, taken by students and employees over the years are unidentified and unmarked. Attributions to photographers include:

Richard Anderson: 138LR

Barton-Gillette Company: 59, 63LL, 138UR, 153U, 172L, 179-3

Blakeslee-Lane Studio: 195

Pete Colhoun: 162L

Fred G. Craft: 158

Willard R. Culver: 151, 152L, 152U, 191LR

James S. Cummings: 11

Bill Denison: 181-7

Jean Doerfler: i, 27, 102, 110, 112, 114U, 117L, 117 U, 121, 125L, 126U, 130L, 133, 134U, 138LL, 148L, 154L, 159L, 168, 169, 174L, 175L, 177LU, 177R, 181-14, 181-15, 181-18, 182-19, 182-25, 182-26, 183-28, 183-30, 183-32, 185-14, 199, 200, 201

Mary Duer: 192L

Leanna Haynie Greene, Class of 1959: 108U, 109, 172UL

Leonard L. Greif: 90

William J. Groeninger: 10L, 13, 23, 26U, 143

David Harp: 111, 181-13, 182-23, back cover

SUGGESTED READING

Nanette Holbein: 180-8

Fred Hollyer: 2, 189U

Joseph Hughes Studio: 10U, 26L, 189L, 193

Cappy Jackson: 184-5, 184-6, 185-7, 185-8, 185-9, 185-12, 185-13

Alain Jaramillo: 120

Vince Lupo: 131UR, 131UL, 131L, 137R, 181-17, 182-27

Walter M. McCardell: 66

Julie Smith Marshall, Class of 1989: 182-23

Maryland Photo Service: 38

Stephen McDaniel: 75, 78, 88, 89, 93, 94, 95, 96, 99L, 99U, 109, 107, 108L, 159U, 163L, 163U, 171L, 176UL, 176LL, 180-9, 180-10, 180-11, 180-12, 198

Lanny Miyamoto: 58, 63U

Jeanne L. Mockard, Class of 1981: 179-4

Joseph W. Mollitor: 73

Todd Olszewski/Baltimore Orioles: 134L

George Upshur Pope: 45

Rich Riggins: 114L

Leo Rosenthal: 40

Matt Roth: 119, 182-22, 185-10, 185-11

Joe Rubino: 182-21

Nancy Sherman: 183-29

Dave Stephens: 115, 124, 125R, 137L, 139U, 139LL, 139LR, 148U, 157L, 157R, 156, 157LL, 162, 163ML, 163MM, 163MR, 175U, 182-20, 183-31

Udel Brothers: 43, 136

David J. Wallace: 184-1

M. E. Warren: 54, 57, 196L

Stuart Zolotorow: 185-15

Albisetti, James C. "American Women's Colleges Through European Eyes, 1865–1914." In *History of Education Quarterly*, Vol. 32, No. 4 (Winter 1992). 439–458. History of Education Society.

Baltimore Hand Book of Colleges, Schools, Libraries, Museums, Halls, & c. Baltimore: Cushings & Bailey, 1876.

Beirne, Rosamond Randall. *Let's Pick the Daisies: The History of the Bryn Mawr School, 1885–1967,* Baltimore: The Bryn Mawr School, 1970.

Bernstein, Barton J. "The Removal of War Production Board Controls on Business, 1944–1946" in *The Business History Review.* Vol. 39, No. 2 (Summer 1965). 243–260. President and Fellows of Harvard College.

Briggs, Ward W. "Gildersleeve and M. Carey Thomas" in *The American Journal of Philology.* Vol. 121, No. 4 (Winter 2000). 629–635. Baltimore: Johns Hopkins University Press.

Chase, Barbara L. "M. Carey Thomas and the 'Friday Night': A Case Study in Female Social Networks and Personal Growth." Master's thesis, Johns Hopkins University, 1990.

Clarke, Edward H., M.D. *Sex in Education; or, A Fair Chance for Girls.* Boston: James R. Osgood and Company, 1875.

DeBare, Ilana. *Where Girls Come First: The Rise, Fall, and Surprising Revival of Girls' Schools,* New York, Tacher/Penguin Books, 2004.

Dobkin, Marjorie Housepian. *The Making of a Feminist: Early Journals and Letters of M. Carey Thomas,* Kent State University Press, 1979.

Eisenmann, Linda. "The Impact of Historical Expectations on Women's Higher Education." The Forum on Public Policy, 2006.

Finch, Edith. *Carey Thomas of Bryn Mawr* New York: Harper & Brothers, 1947.

Flexner, Helen Thomas. *A Quaker Childhood.* New Haven: Yale University Press, 1940.

Hall, Clayton Colman, ed. *Baltimore, Its History and Its People.* Volumes I-III. New York and Chicago, Lewis Historical Publishing Co., 1912.

Hamilton, Alice. *Exploring the Dangerous Trades: The Autobiography of Alice Hamilton,* Boston: Little, Brown and Company, 1943.

Hamm, Thomas D. *The Transformation of American Quakerism: Orthodox Friends, 1800–1907,* Bloomington and Indianapolis: Indiana University Press, 1988.

Harvard University. *General Education in a Free Society: Report of the Harvard Committee.* Cambridge, MA: Harvard University Press, 1946.

Horowitz, Helen Lefkowitz. *The Power and Passion of M. Carey Thomas,* New York: Alfred A. Knopf, 1994.

SUGGESTED READING

Horowitz, Helen L. "'Nous Autres': Reading, Passion, and the Creation of M. Carey Thomas," in *Journal of American History*, Vol. 79 (June 1992). 68-95.

Horowitz, Helen L. *Alma Mater: Design and Experience in the Women's Colleges from Their Nineteenth Century Beginnings to the 1930s* New York: Alfred A. Knopf, 1984.

Leonard, Fred Eugene. *Pioneers of Modern Physical Training*. New York: Association Press, 1919.

Mackinnon, Alison. "Educated doubt: women, religion and the challenge of higher education, c. 1870–1920" in *Women's History Review*, Vol. 7 No.2, 1998. 241–259.

Novey, Joelle Gail. "'One Aim and Concentrated Purpose': M. Carey Thomas as Daring Visionary and Flawed Reformer" in *The Concord Review*, Vol. 7 No.3, Spring 1997.

Power, Garrett. "High Society: The Building Height Limitation on Baltimore's Mt. Vernon Place" in *Maryland Historical Magazine*, Vol. 79, No. 3, Fall 1984.

Reid, Doris Fielding. *Edith Hamilton: An Intimate Portrait*, New York: W.W. Norton & Company, 1967.

Rossiter, Margaret W., "Doctorates for American Women, 1868-1907" in *History of Education Quarterly*, Vol. 22, No. 2, (Summer 1982), 159-183.

Rossiter, Margaret W. "Women Scientists in America" in *Bulletin of the American Academy of Arts and Sciences*, Vol. 36, No. 6 (March 1983), 10-16.

Rupp, Leila J. "'Imagine My Surprise': Women's Relationships in Historical Perspective" in *Frontiers*, Vol. V, No. 3, 1981.

Sander, Kathleen Waters. *Mary Elizabeth Garrett: Society and Philanthropy in the Gilded Age*, Baltimore: Johns Hopkins University Press, 2008.

Sicherman, Barbara. *Alice Hamilton: A Life in Letters*, Cambridge, MA: Harvard University Press, 1984.

Sicherman, Barbara, ed. *Notable American Women: the modern period*, Cambridge, MA: Harvard University Press, 1980.

Sicherman, Barbara. "Reading and Ambition: M. Carey Thomas and Female Heroism" in *American Quarterly*, Vol. 45, No. 1 (March 1993), 73-103.

Sicherman. "Connecting Lives: Women and Reading, Then and Now" in *Women in Print*, Madison: University of Wisconsin Press, 2006, 3-24.

Solomon, Barbara Miller. *In the Company of Educated Women: A History of Women and Higher Education in America*, New Haven: Yale University Press, 1985.

Thomas, M. Carey. *"Address"* in *University of Pennsylvania: Addresses Delivered At the Opening of the Graduate Department For Women on Wednesday, May 4th, 1892*. Philadelphia: Allen, Lane & Scott's Printing House, 1892. University of Pennsylvania Archives.

Thomas, M. Carey. "Should the Higher Education of Women Differ from that of Men?," *Educational Review* 21 (1901).

Thomas, M. Carey. *Women's College and University Education: Address Delivered at the Quarter-Centennial Meeting of the Association of Collegiate Alumnae, Boston, November 6, 1907*. Reprinted from the Educational Review, New York, January 1908.

Welch, William H. "Contribution of Bryn Mawr College to the Higher Education of Women" in *Science*. Vol. 56, No. 1436 (July 7, 1922). 1-8. American Association for the Advancement of Science.

Welsh, Lillian. *Reminiscences of Thirty Years in Baltimore*. Baltimore: The Norman, Remington Co., 1925.

Zschoche, Sue. "Dr. Clarke Revisited: Science, True Womanhood, and Female Collegiate Education" in *History of Education Quarterly*, Vol. 29, No. 4 (Winter 1989). 545-569.